The Effects of Trauma

And How to Deal with It

Jim Banks

with chapters by Pat Banks, Becca Wineka, and
By Jennifer Webb

"I broke the fangs of the unrighteous and made him drop his prey from his teeth." – Job 29:17 (ESV)

House of Healing Ministries
P.O. Box 60, Campbellsville, KY 42719
http://www.houseofhealingministries.org

2nd Printing – 2012
ISBN-13: 9780983260608
ISBN-10: 0983260605

Please note that House of Healing Ministries' publishing style capitalizes certain
pronouns in Scripture that refer to the Father, Son, and Holy Spirit, and may differ
from some Bible publisher's styles.

Take note that the name satan and related names are not capitalized. We choose
not to acknowledge him, even to the point of violating grammatical rules.

Editing, Formatting, and Artwork:
Cover photography - "Sun Reflecting on Lake McDonald, Glacier National Park."
Copyright ©2011, Becca Wineka. All Rights Reserved.
Brooke Jack, Editor
Joshua Jack, Creative Director

Table of Contents

Foreword

God's grace is evident in this supernatural download of scientific, evidence-based understanding of how we are made...it is scientifically, theoretically, and biblically sound. The systematic process of release and reconciliation is powerful, and is both spiritual and physiological, even occurring at a molecular level! It is a testimony of God's persistent pursuit to see our spirit, soul, and body restored and of His Love's beautiful, unrelenting chase and steadfast jealousy over our lives (Song of Solomon 8:6-7).

Ashley E Dorough, PhD
Clinical Health Psychologist

The healing ministry in the Church has been going through a growth process. One of the most noticeable, recent changes is the understanding that no one model of healing is sufficient to help bring a person to healing. Jim Banks has remarkably illustrated this integrated healing model in his new book, *The Effects of Trauma and How to Deal With It*. The book is a must for all who desire to minister to the hurting.

Dr. Paul Cox
Aslan's Place

Testimonies

I've used the [Trauma] Prayer [Process] with two people with outstanding results. One was a very mature, devoted Christian leader with a prophetic gifting, always rallying the troops to go higher in God. One day, she was in an auto accident. Two weeks later, she began to have crying jags. She said she felt so vulnerable and afraid (very unlike her!). I didn't get through all of the prayer, as God took us on a little diversion, but the main points we covered. In another two weeks, she reported a miraculous deliverance from the fear and vulnerability! She's recommending it to others.

I also prayed with another strong Christian who had suffered loss upon loss, and the results have again been miraculous. The last session was six hours on the phone, but we made it through, using your format with a few little variations as the Lord led. Thanks so much for the work you did, putting the prayer together in written form. – **J.B.**

Many years ago I was told by our family physician at the time that the cause of my aching muscles and morning stiffness was due to Fibromyalgia. I have had some relief through the years from my own as well as other's prayers. Several years later, I was diagnosed with Osteoarthritis and two years ago had replacement surgery on my left knee. After hearing of House of Healing Ministries and of Jim and Pat Banks about 2 months ago, I have studied the downloads from their web site (houseofhealingministries.org). I had already prayed for myself to break the effects of word curses, especially and specifically written medical diagnoses. Recently, I read the [Trauma Prayer Process]. I immediately recognized the truth of the concept, read the teaching and prayed for and over myself using the guidelines. This was June 10, 2010. As of today, June 16, 2010, I have slept peacefully with no aches, pains, or morning stiffness. As of today, I have no pain in my neck, shoulder joints, thumbs, wrists or ankles, all of which have been a constant source of pain and sleep disturbance in the past. All Praise and Glory to God, and "thank you!" to Jim Banks for being obedient to report what he (and Pat) are discovering as they faithfully minster. - **Judy H**.

The following is a testimony of a 3 month-old who cried virtually continually since birth. The mom was frantic and was at the end of her rope. Pat [Banks] prayed the Trauma Prayer Process over him and this was the response:

"Hi Pat...I talked to E.J. this morning and Isaac is sleeping like a baby. She said that he wakes up to eat and goes right back to sleep! Yeah God!"

As you journey through this book, also find the testimonies between the chapters. Not only do they reinforce that God is truly the Healer, but also solidify that overcoming the enemy is through the "blood of the Lamb and the word of their [the saints] testimony."

Introduction

You have extraordinary power to reestablish justice and make a real difference in the lives of those whom the enemy took unfair advantage of during childhood.

I want to take you on a little journey that will open your eyes to some things which are necessary for you to enter into the fullness of your own personal Kingdom destiny that God has prepared for you, and will help you assist those you are ministering to. What you hold in your hand is the result of a journey I started with the Lord a couple of years ago when a dozen or more single women, all thirty and under, began coming to me complaining that they were being awakened repeatedly during the night by tormenting dreams and visions, and the appearance of demons in their workplaces and homes. Several of them stated, "This is what it was like when I was a kid."

I prayed against all sorts of things that I had learned about over the years, but nothing ever seemed to eradicate it all. I began to look for deeper things and potential strategies of the enemy greater than the ramification of just a single incident.

As I began to pursue the clues I was given, two things became abundantly clear. First was the sudden re-appearance of spiritual gifting. The vast majority of these girls were born with what is termed as a "Seer" gifting; in short, the ability to see into the spirit realm as clearly as though it were the natural realm that you and I interact with daily. They not only took in everything that you and I are familiar with, but were also awake to the negative (demonic) activity in the spirit realm as well. The demons that they saw naturally as children created such fear in them that they had all determined to turn that gifting off permanently. Here they were in their mid to late 20's and their gifting was inexplicably turned back on again, with much the same result, and they were tired of it.

On a spiritual level, this is the equivalent of spiritual identity. In this case, these girls had been born as the spiritual eyes of the Body of Christ, and yet there were no spiritual mothers and fathers around to take them on into maturity by helping them learn how to use and manage the gift they were given. Since the fear it engendered was so significant for them, they chose (at the enemy's urging) to turn it off – deny who they were created to be.

Secondly, something that was common for each them was the experience of some form of trauma fairly early on in life, many of them sexual molestation. The force of the trauma had also altered something significant in them related to identity, and somehow the combination of the reactivated spiritual gifting and the recurrence of tormenting dreams was either related to or a direct product of it.

Personal Identity

Personal identity is always found in, but sometimes locked away in, the human spirit.

Ephesians 1:3-4 (KJV) states, *"Blessed be the God and Father of our Lord Jesus Christ, who hath blessed us with every spiritual blessing in the heavenly places in Christ: even as he chose us in him before the foundation of the world, that we should be holy and without blemish before him in love."*

Ephesians 2:10 (KJV) declares, *"For we are his workmanship, created in Christ Jesus unto good works, which God hath before ordained that we should walk in them."*

Let me restate these three verses in one: *"There were good works created (ordained or established) for you and I to perform before the foundation of the world, and we've been given every spiritual blessing required to execute them."*

You may be asking, "So, what does this have to do with personal identity?" Great question! Let's take a look at some additional scriptures to find the answer.

In Genesis 1:26, the Bible says that you and I were created in the image of God. In John 4:24, Jesus proclaimed, *"God is a Spirit: and they that worship him must worship in spirit and truth."* Later on in 1 Thessalonians 5:23, Paul says, *"And the God of peace himself sanctify you wholly; and may your spirit and soul and body be preserved entire, without blame at the coming of our Lord Jesus Christ."*

What God has established for us is the fact that we are principally spirit beings, which is why Paul says at the conclusion of his letters to the Galatians, Philippians, his second to Timothy, and from Philemon, *"The grace of the Lord Jesus Christ be with your spirit."* According to 1 Thessalonians 5:23, there is an order to the way we are to live our lives: our human spirit subjected to the spirit of God that dwells within us, our human spirit ruling over our soul (defined as our mind, will and emotions), which in turn is to rule over our body.

According to the combined statement of Ephesians 1:3-4 and 2:10 above, the works that were prepared for us to perform before the foundation of the world are spiritual works to be performed by spirit people using the spiritual blessings (gifts) He (God) has provided for us in Christ Jesus. That is the bottom line of destiny and purpose.

What are the works?

First, some background is needed. There was a war in heaven:

Isaiah 14:12-15 (KJV): *"How art thou fallen from heaven, O Lucifer, son of the morning! how art thou cut down to the ground, which didst weaken the nations! For thou hast said in thine heart, I will ascend into heaven, I will exalt my throne above the stars of God: I will sit also upon the mount of the congregation, in the sides of the north: I will ascend above the heights of the clouds; I will be like the most High. Yet thou shalt be brought down to hell, to the sides of the pit."*

Lucifer was cast out of heaven to earth. Jesus, the faithful and true witness, declared in Luke 10:18 (KJV), *"I beheld Satan as lightning fall from heaven."*

There are two things that coincide here from these two passages. From Isaiah 12:14 we see the result of Lucifer's fall to the earth, *"which didst weaken the nations!"* Note the emphasis. It was very apparent to Isaiah when he had this vision that earth was a decidedly different place after Lucifer's banishment. Note also the words. The Hebrew word translated here as "weaken" is from a primitive root word meaning, "prostrate, overthrow, decay, waste away."

Let me restate these three verses in one: "There were good works created (ordained or established) for you and I to perform before the foundation of the world, and we've been given every spiritual blessing required to execute them."

This state of continual decline is met by Jesus declaring to his disciples in Luke 10:19-20, *"Behold, I give unto you power to tread on serpents and scorpions, and over all the power of the enemy: and nothing shall by any means hurt you. Notwithstanding in this rejoice not, that the spirits are subject unto you; but rather rejoice, because your names are written in heaven."*

God is redemptive in all His ways. Therefore, before there was a need for anything on this planet to be redeemed, there was ample provision. 1 Peter 1:18-20 declares that the lamb was slain for you and me before the foundation of the world. Before you sinned, there was the provision of forgiveness. Before you owed a debt you could not pay, there was provision. Before you needed a savior, there was a sacrifice.

When Jesus said to His disciples, "I saw Lucifer bite the dust," followed by, *"I give unto you power to tread on serpents and scorpions, and over all the power of the enemy: and nothing shall by any means hurt you,"* Jesus was establishing His right and His authority to redeem the earth and all its inhabitants. Since Jesus never saw demons as anything bigger than creepy-crawly things, and satan was to be under His feet, He referred to them as scorpions and snakes. Harmful? Yes, but with the Balm of Gilead, not deadly.

Why do I say not deadly? Because in Genesis 1:26, God created us in His image, his likeness. His word says He never sleeps nor slumbers – then neither does our spirit. That is how David could say in Psalm 139 that his spirit (heart) instructed him on his bed while he slept. At night, my soul is in a temporary state of hibernation while my body is being restored/re-invigorated/re-energized for the events of the coming day, but my spirit doesn't shut down. It can turn its face to the Lord and receive everything it needs for the coming day – if so inclined.

Further, since we are created in His image, and He is spirit, and He had neither beginning nor end, it is quite likely that our human spirits are eternal as well. To my mind, we have to be since he created us to dwell with Him forever in the hereafter of heaven. That's why he called us a new creation – that whom we have become is not recycled.

I think that concept is reinforced by Jeremiah 1:4-5 (KJV): *"Then the word of the LORD came unto me, saying, 'Before I formed thee in the belly I knew thee; and before thou camest forth out of the womb I sanctified thee, and I ordained thee a prophet unto the nations'."* The Hebrew word in verse 5 translated "knew" is "yada." It is the same word used when Adam "knew" Eve and she conceived a son, and Abraham "knew" Sarah and became pregnant. It carries with it the inference that there is more than cognitive or even figurative knowledge, such as "I recognize you to be spirit # 4,578,692." It infers that He (God) had some sort of intimate, interactive knowledge of us gained experientially. If that is true, then the hunger we have for God, a god, is such that some beneficial relationship with authority is really in some way a desire to fulfill a distant memory. It is my personal belief that we too knew God. That in this place of pre-history we beheld His beauty, His majesty, and felt His love, spirit to Spirit.

There apparently came a day when God created us. In doing so, He chose to build into us whatever was needed to be effective in three arenas:

1. To be fit for and effective in the Kingdom of God.
   "Fear not, little flock; for it is your Father's good pleasure to give you the kingdom." Luke 12:32

2. To be responsive to God in a manner that he can work in and through us.
   "For it is God which worketh in you both to will and to do of his good pleasure." Philippians 2:13

3. To fulfill the specific desires that He has placed in our hearts which are connected to identity and purpose.
   "Delight thyself also in the LORD; and he shall give thee the desires of thine heart." Psalm 37:4

I want to key in on # 3 above because I believe that it is very important to understand the implications of it, both for ourselves and those to whom we minister. If you recall from Jeremiah 1:5, God declared that before Jeremiah had been placed in his mother's womb, He had already determined that Jeremiah was going to be a prophet to the nations (destiny or calling) and God had sanctified (set him apart) him for that specific task. This is where Psalm 37:4 comes in.

I believe that one day in Heaven there was a council held between the Father, Son and Holy Spirit. They knew in great detail what Jeremiah was set to be, but they had to install some things in him in order for him to ever want to get close to doing it. For each of us, including Jeremiah, they had to install a specific mix of talents, abilities, intellect, personality, skills, desires, dislikes, wants and needs. They even installed the way you perceive things, the way you view problems and opportunities, the way you think, your temperament, and your spiritual gifts, each of which were empowered by a hidden set of desires or drive to be fulfilled. The total mix of all these ingredients I call "identity." It is that special mix that makes you uniquely you. It was the Father's delight to make only one you, because only you, with that unique collection of expressions of gifts, talents, acquired skills, wants, dreams and desires could perform that pre-determined set of "good works" (Ephesians 2:10) that He created you to perform before the foundation of the world.

It is also my guess that there was another party to all of God's magnificent creative display the day you were made – Lucifer. He was probably there applauding each and every exquisite choice the Father made as He lovingly fashioned you for His purposes, silently taking note of everything Father did – even the *"vessels made for honor and dishonor"* (Romans 9:21).

Once Lucifer was "shown the door" – make that, "given the left foot of fellowship" – and found himself doing a serious face-plant on planet earth, he was really mad! Mad at God, mad at the earth, mad at man! He immediately set about to show God a thing or two about His prized possessions, the people He fashioned for Himself for "His good pleasure!" Thus, he tricked Adam and Eve, the first man and woman sent to earth to rectify (redeem) the damage Lucifer had done when he was sentenced to earth, into turning over to him authority over the earth. Through that broken and sinful pair, God established a race of people to call His own and through them brought a second Adam (the first natural, the second spiritual), Jesus, to redeem earth and man.

In his wrath, Lucifer knew how each of us was created and probably what we were created for. (Sometimes you can tell a great deal about a person's real destiny and purpose for being here by simply identifying where and how they have been attacked.) Consequently, that was what he went after – identity. If you don't know who you are and why you are here, everything's an option for you. That's similar to the old saying, *"If you don't know where you're going, any road will take you there."* Most of us know the pain of winding up in a place we had no business being, and the arduous task of getting back on course.

Therefore, satan's attack is launched at who you are – your identity. He doesn't need to assign a horde of demons to your case to mess you up. He starts with your ancestors, persuading them to fall into all sorts of sin and entanglements. They build mental ideologies and structures of thoughts about why things are the way they are (called their truth) and teach them to their children, so in time, they become your truth, even if it has no resemblance to the real truth and reality of life at all.

Then there are the direct assaults against you, when you are at your weakest and most vulnerable. These include vicious wounds like death of a parent(s), divorce, abandonment, sexual molestation, rape, sodomy, rejection, poverty, mental and physical abuse, and emotional abandonment. Out of these experiences, we build walls out of fear of experiencing further hurt and pain. They in turn keep out everything, including the love we so desperately desire. Trauma occurs and the enemy is there to feed us more lies about ourselves.

Over time, we find ourselves in a place of isolation and disconnection, with a heart that is shut down and cold as stone. We want life, but everything seems to be a poor imitation. The enemy has us right where he wants us: we don't know who we are and have no idea why we're here – no sense of destiny or purpose. We've lost our identity.

We have all been there on one level or another. To those who have been horrifically abused and traumatized, it feels like a lifetime and there appears to be no hope for a comeback.

When Jesus appeared on the scene, in whom was all the fullness of God Himself, he established the fact that there was a new Sheriff in town! He went about deputizing (giving authority to) all who would follow him. To those deputies, He gave the 'dunamis' power of the Holy Spirit to kick spiritual butt and take names, to break the power of sin (generational and otherwise) off man, to break the power of the defilement of sin off the land and set it free to be a blessing to man, and to re-establish kingdom order in the house!

Now you know why the enemy is after your personal identity.

The good news is, as hard as this seems to be on us, God has a plan and He's not concerned about achieving His heart's purposes at all. He has secretly been preparing a mighty army of folks who have been through hell and have survived to help others. These folks may or may not be in a church, some of them still are, but they have a couple of things in common: they love God, and they love people in a practical manner that requires them to give of themselves. All in all, a magnificent fulfillment of Matthew 22:37-40.

The good news is that these folks are gathering together to form healing communities of varying sizes and descriptions, from a few folks who get together once a week to pray for the sick, to dozens who meet all over the city doing inner healing, deliverance, working with the abused, the drug addicted, the abandoned, the widows and the orphans, the prisons, and the half-way houses and shelters across America. My wife and I have been privileged these last few years to help establish some and nourish several others all across the south. It's fun to watch God do His thing!

One last word

Before we launch off into reestablishing destiny and purpose by recovering personal identity, I want to clarify what was written earlier in this treatise about destiny and purpose. Jesus said in John 10 that He came that you might have life, and life abundant. Certainly destiny and purpose being fulfilled is all about life. But, there is more to life than doing the works that were established for us to perform before the foundation of the world. Life is all about relationship.

In Matthew 19, Jesus is asked by a young, performance-oriented, rich guy what else he needs to check off his list of things to do in order to achieve eternal life. Jesus slaps him upside the head with his retort of, *"Well ... if you would enter into life, keep all these commandments ...(v.17)."* All the commandments Jesus gave him were not about what not to do (don't lie, don't steal, don't covet), they were the foundational elements of basic relationships, that is, how you treat your neighbors, your employees, your fellow synagogue attendees, etc. In other words, Jesus was saying that one of the chief ways of insuring that you are qualified to enter the Kingdom of Heaven is to be certain you qualify as a good friend, a neighbor, a son, a brother or a sister. How you live before God is seen in how you live before men and vice versa.

God is really into personal relationships. Why else would he say in Matthew 5:23 that if you're in church and you remember that somebody has something against you, leave and go make it right? Or, in Matthew 6:14-15, that if you want forgiveness from God, you have to forgive.

Some time ago we had a series of young people come through our office door expressing that they were frustrated that life seemed to be passing them by. They were afraid that they were missing their destiny. I assured them that it was not at all likely that they would miss what God had for them. But just to make sure, I began a word study on the word "destiny" in scripture. What I found was surprising. There is only one verse in the New Testament translated as "destiny" and it declares that we are "destined" to become conformed to the image of Jesus Christ (Romans 8:29). When I looked at the meaning of destiny, I was even more surprised because that word carries with it the connotation of fate. In other words, being conformed to the image of Christ is going to happen.

A single verse with reference to destiny and then, by contrast, the balance of the New Testament was written entirely about relationship. It ought to be apparent to us that relationships are the key to real life, but somehow we still prize independence and eschew connectedness. For most of us, it is the pain of trauma, derived from those whom we were supposed to be able to trust, thrust upon us, which has left us unable to trust and enter fully into healthy relationships. Conversely, it is through healthy relationships that we will recover our identity and experience the abundant life of joy-filled, meaningful relationships.

It is to that end that this Trauma Prayer Process was written: recovery of God-given identity. It is only one piece of the entire puzzle, but an important one. Have fun with it, add to it as the Holy Spirit gives revelation and spread it far and wide.

"Bless you and Pat for all you guys do. Thank you for sharing with me your wisdom. I have your book in my purse and the Trauma Prayer on my iPod. I enjoyed your testimony on the young people you ministered to who were seers. I'm a seer too and had some of the same experiences. Every time things get wacky, all I have to do is put that Trauma Prayer on and pray in agreement with it and I sleep so good – no bad dreams."

The Problem

Psalm 34:19a "Many are the afflictions of the righteous. . ."

In John 16:33b (NASB) Jesus said - *"In the world you have tribulation; but be of good cheer, I have overcome the world."* Note that He didn't say "will have," as though it were some time in the future, or "may have," as though it were not certain, or "possibly have," as though there were a "tribulation lottery" which you might not win; but He said that you have it now (in some form).

The Greek word for **tribulation** is "thlipsis" which means pressure *(literally or figuratively): - afflicted, (-tion), anguish, burdened, persecution, tribulation, trouble.*[1]

Note that this verse clearly states that we will all have it. Everybody experiences it one way or another. Trauma and tribulation, like beauty, are in the eye of the beholder. Not everyone experiences it with the same intensity or results. Multiple children growing up in the same house and experiencing the same event will find that it registers rather differently with each child. Some will not even realize that the event was traumatic. But for those who do, there is no doubt.

According to the web site David Baldwin's Trauma Information Pages, a web resource for all things trauma, "Traumatic experiences shake the foundations of our beliefs about safety, and shatter our assumptions of trust."[2]

Those that suffer from some physical and/or emotional difficulty have usually experienced significant emotional and/or physical trauma at some point in their lives. This has detrimentally affected their ability to recover from the normal, but difficult circumstances of life, and return to a state where they remain stable. Removing the physical effects of trauma can greatly help an individual achieve or regain the capacity to heal and grow in many areas. It can also eliminate the daily torment of the long term effects of trauma, both emotionally and physically.

"In the healing process, the crucial issue is building enough capacity to stay relationally connected to God over a sufficient amount of time for us to allow

the process to be completed."[3] I believe that part of the process of helping someone build that capacity is achieved through removing as many of the various effects of trauma as possible.

Unfortunately, trauma can affect us on many levels - emotional, spiritual and physical. Medically, the understanding and treatment of the effects of trauma has been limited primarily to the emotional aspects of it. Consequently, medication has been the sole response to the problem and seems to have been relegated to insulating the victim from experiencing the resulting pain.

Traditional medicine recognizes that our bodies have many identifiable, but little understood, capabilities. One of them is the retention of the memory of trauma at a cellular level, but treatment has not been particularly effective in reversing its effects.

Symptoms

Human response to trauma can be experienced over quite a range of symptoms from mild to chronic. The following represent the most significant and are generally ascribed to sufferers of Post-traumatic-stress disorder:

- Intrusive, upsetting memories of the event
- Flashbacks (acting or feeling like the event is happening again)

- Nightmares or disturbing dreams (either of the event or of other frightening things; violent or sexually defiling)
- Feelings of intense distress when reminded of the trauma
- Intense physical reactions to reminders of the event (e.g. pounding heart, rapid breathing, nausea, muscle tension, sweating)
- Avoiding activities, places, thoughts, or feelings that remind you of the trauma
- Inability to remember important aspects of the trauma
- Loss of interest in activities and life in general
- Feeling detached from others and emotionally numb
- Sense of a limited future
- Interrupted sleep and skewed sleep patterns
- Irritability or outbursts of anger
- Difficulty concentrating
- Hyper-vigilance
- Exaggerated fright response or being easily startled
- Anger and irritability
- Guilt, shame, or self-blame
- Substance abuse
- Depression and hopelessness
- Suicidal thoughts and feelings
- Feeling alienated and alone

- Feelings of mistrust and betrayal
- Headaches, stomach problems, chest pain

Spiritual Significance

A colleague of mine has an understanding that trauma itself is a specific scheme of the enemy to gain access to us for purposes of future torment and emotional torture. His take on it is that when Jesus was on the cross, the darkness that overtook the scene that day was neither a storm, nor the aftermath of a localized earth quake, as many Biblical scholars have tried to reason. But instead, it was every demon in hell coming to take its last best shot at Him as he hung there helplessly; a barrage of intentional torments and torture. It is little wonder that his death took comparatively so little time on the cross.

Consequently, Jesus' death on the cross was complete atonement in another aspect of human life in that He took upon Himself all the trauma, torture and torment intended for you and me. We do not have to suffer (*relive*) that again. Once was enough. It is my colleague's belief that the principle behind this scheme of the enemy is to cause trauma before the cross became effective in the life of an individual for one of two purposes: 1) make it difficult for a person to enter into their full identity, and 2) for the purpose of causing future torment.

Note: Please do not read into this something I did not say. When I said, "We do not have to suffer that again," I did not say that we do not have to suffer ever again because of Christ's substitutionary death. Obviously, anyone who has lived on this planet at least a decade will tell you that is not true. Scripture certainly backs that up (John 16:33). We are specifically saying that we do not have to repeatedly re-suffer torment due to trauma.

The only way that "before the cross became effective" is remotely possible is to remove some portion of the individual to another dimension, time, space or place and hold it captive there.[4]

Dr. Tom Hawkins, founder of Restoration in Christ Ministries[5], has noted as a result of ministry to numerous SRA victims that portions of their identity/being can be stuck/captured/imprisoned/delayed in other dimensions, times or spaces through intentionally enforced trauma, which to my mind confirms the assertion that a trauma victim's identity can be messed with by intentionally introducing, or taking advantage of, events that effectively freezes some portion of the individual.

Jesus' death on the cross was complete atonement in another aspect of human life in that He took upon Himself all the trauma, torture and torment intended for you and me.

You and I live in a multi-dimensional world but are generally only cognizant of four dimensions: *height, width, depth and time.* Theoretical physicists, folks like Albert Einstein, have been working on a series of theories since the 20's in an attempt to reduce them to a single equation (or series of equations) which encompasses all theoretical equations (such as Gravity, Einstein's Theory of Relativity and the concepts of Quantum Mechanics). That single elegant mathematical equation would encompass and explain the operation and interaction of everything, which many have termed 'The God Factor." There have been a series of five string theories postulated in an effort to make this all work together, and as it turns out, these theories work quite well in an environment where there are at least 11 dimensions. This has come to be known as the subsequent amped-up version, Superstring Theory.[6] One set of these theories only works universally if there are as many as 23 dimensions.

In the eleventh dimension, all of the five string theories, general relativity, and quantum mechanics knit together forming a web of relationships. This relational web which occurs "looks" mathematically and theoretically like a membrane as it is viewed from the perspective of the eleventh dimension. Hence, this theory is called "M" theory for membrane. Out of this has developed a new proto-science called "Brane Cosmology."[7]   In this view of the universe, our visible, knowable universe is contained within these membranes and thought to exist inside a higher dimensional space.

Altered DNA

You and I are made in the image of God. God is light, and consequently, we are children of light.[8] Scientists tell us that if each organ is broken down to the lowest common denominator, it will all be a similar type of cell; same DNA as the whole person, but encoded such that it will perform well within the context of that organ. If we break that cell down further, we find a number of atoms. Each atom can be further reduced to its component parts: neutron, proton(s) and electron(s). These elements vibrate at a specific frequency which is in accord with the individual's DNA. Scientists further tell us that if each individual's DNA strand is un-twisted, it can be played as a melody on a piano (more vibrations). This subject matter referred to as "bioinformatics."[9]

> **You and I are made in the image of God and God is light, and consequently, we are children of light.**

When the enemy messes with us through our own sinful activity or cursed generational (family) issues, our DNA can be altered by attaching junk to the strand.[10] Through trauma, our "song" can be changed from a major key to a minor one, simply by slightly altering our frequency. Although our DNA can't be altered and our DNA is passed on to our children, things riding on it can have a profound ability to affect the next generation. How can that be done? By removing one small part of us to another domain or dimension.

As a consequence, I am further convinced that trauma can also be a generational issue. Experience has taught a major contributor to the inner healing field that some traumas can be passed on from mother to child during nursing creating a form of secondary trauma in the child.

Arrested Development

Most of us are familiar with walking up to the check-out counter at your local grocery store and being greeted by a cashier in their thirties who speaks to you in the voice of a 10 year-old. Apparently, something significant happened to that person at the age of 10 and a portion of them was frozen at that age; their development in that area ceased. I cannot say with any certainty that this is a perfect example of the ravages of trauma, but dealing with it in the manner described herein, along with resolving the associated emotional wounds, may be one of the keys to releasing them to achieve full maturity in several areas. It may never change their voice, but it will enable major changes in other areas.

We ministered to a child of seven who was developmentally scored as operating on the level of a three year old. His parents complained of a very brief attention span, lack of attachment, easy arousal of anger, and limited communication, as he was minimally verbal with them, preferring to use grunts, groans, and gestures, and was never verbal around strangers. We had his parents repent of generational sins on both sides of the family and prayed the trauma prayer process over him while he played. Thirty days afterward, his parents reported that incidents of anger had subsided significantly, he was voluntarily demonstrating acts of attachment principally by sitting in father or mother's lap, and his vocabulary had risen by about 25%. To their great delight, there were only a few remnants of the grunt, groan and gesture communication style.

There are elements of arrested development that are easy to overlook in adults who have experienced significant trauma as a child:

- Difficulty in maintaining long-term relationships
- Lack of trust
- Poor or inability to attach
- Lack of problem resolutions skills

One of the key factors in survival for sufferers of long-term trauma is a highly developed ability to live in denial which is very problematic for long-term relationships. When one spouse can easily disconnect in situations where there is tension, communication begins to head south in a hurry. In any relationship, be it with employers, spouses, or neighbors, problems large and small will need to be resolved. Consequently, communication issues will surface. The spouse who has a tendency to live in denial and has never been forced to resolve problems in a healthy manner will always choose to disconnect, forcing the other spouse to deal with issues they may not be qualified to handle, or create issues for the couple because they were not handled as the retreating spouse would have liked. This results in a "lose-lose" situation, and is one of the ways the enemy side tracks destiny and purpose.

Another element that is problematic for many individuals has to do with attachment styles. Dependent upon which school of thought you buy into, humans have been generally identified to have one of three or four attachment styles. One version of the school of four, names them as:

- **Secure**. Individuals with 'secure' attachment styles would report that they are comfortable with others needing them, that they can get emotionally close to others and enjoy it, their close relationships are warm and responsive, and they don't get worked up over being rejected, nor do they expect to be rejected.
- **Anxious-preoccupied** would say of themselves that they need to be emotionally close with others and are uncomfortable when they're not. If they are not it is generally their fault. They tend to be clingy and impulsive.
- **Dismissive-avoidant**. These folks would say they like being independent and are comfortable without close emotional connections. They are frequently accused of avoiding relationships.

- **Fearful-avoidant** would say, "I want to be close but have difficulty trusting." They desire close relationships but are not certain they can handle them and don't want to expect too much. There is a pronounced fear of being hurt.

Obviously, we would all like to think that we desire to be in the 'secure' category, but those who have experienced significant trauma as children or young adults find themselves in the double bind of hoping they can someday find themselves in the anxious category, but live out of the restrictive end of fearful. The internal turmoil it creates makes them miserable - wanting to trust and feel connected, but not daring to out of fear of additional suffering.

The latter three in this list of attachment styles can live in denial, but none of them can really touch the extraordinary capabilities of the dismissive to do so. They will admit to wanting close emotional relationships, but are comfortable living without them. If you betray or significantly wound them, they will simply write you off as "no longer existing." Poof, you're gone. I have laughingly referred to myself, being firmly fixed in this category, as having an exceptionally well-developed case of instantaneous voluntarily dissociation – something to be envied. It worked well for me early on, but has been nothing but trouble for us in our marriage.

Fortunately for us, about 15 or 16 years ago, we made a decision to go somewhere for ministry for 3 or four days annually, whether we need it or not. We still feel like we still have a ways to go to get where we want to be, both individually and as a couple. Some habits and paradigms of thought die hard. It is encouraging for both of us to know that our partner is as committed to working out the kinks in our relationship as we are, evidenced by the fact that they are facing the issues head on along with us.

The Inability to Sustain Healing

Many of you are acquainted with someone that you have worked with over some period of time, who seems to be progressing very well. When separated from them for a period of 45 days or more, you are surprised to find that they were as bad, or worse off, than they were when you first began to work with them. I believe that one of the potential reasons this occurs is due to some vital portion of that person, needful for sustaining progress, has been disconnected from them, imprisoned somewhere in the dimensions. This may happen as our client denies, or chose to disconnect from, a portion of themselves that they find unattractive, not socially acceptable, or makes them feel vulnerable.

Although this may not be the appropriate venue for it, I feel compelled to state that because trauma is such a universal experience it may well be one of the foundational issues that we need to gain revelation and understanding of in order to see more physical healings in response to prayer. I have only prayed in this direction a few times with inconclusive results.

Having operated a healing room for over seven years (as of this writing), it is common knowledge that approximately 85% of the physical issues we humans seek medical attention for have their roots in either emotional or spiritual issues. When resolved, the physical issue is either healed immediately or healing proceeds rapidly. Release of the effects of trauma needs to be a tool we commonly apply when praying for the ill and infirm.

We have been meeting with "T" and "C" in preparation for this ministry they are launching. The deeper I got into it, the more dread seemed to be filling me up. It didn't seem to affect the rest of my body – just my heart.

Last night on the way home from our meeting, I started to have heart palpitations. My heart just started racing like I had run a mile, and then it started skipping one out of every four beats. I thought, "Dear God, I am having a dang heart attack!" and "By gosh, I don't have time for this!" I started praying in tongues, which held it at bay, but as soon as I would "relax" my stand, it would immediately come back. I couldn't find your book when I got home. "B" was asleep and it was hard to wake him up. He got up and prayed for me and that held it at bay, but I knew it was still there. I prayed over myself and bound everything I could think of. I think I even prayed the "if I die before I wake" prayer, too!

This morning, it started about an hour after I got up. You sent the prayer. I prayed it and it immediately stopped -- took me about 1-1/2 hours to go through it. Thank you, JESUS! And, thank you guys! I so appreciate you putting this book together!"

Freedom from Trauma

Jesus' substitutionary death in our behalf says we do not have to suffer the subsequent torment that trauma victims usually report.

A pplying the principles of Jesus Christ's Atonement to the issues of the effects and the residue of trauma in the life of a trauma victim will begin to restore the proper order. Jesus' substitutionary death in our behalf says we do not have to suffer the subsequent torment that trauma victims usually report. This does not mean that we'll never have to experience "tribulation" ever again. That's what we get for living in this neighborhood. It simply means that we can cut off the tormenting effects of trauma so that we won't have to relive it time and again whenever something happens that reminds us of it.

Ministry to victims of trauma

1. Interview

Through specific questions, usually an interview, determine the traumatic events for the client from childhood into adulthood (physical, emotional, spiritual, and sexual). Inquire about such things as divorce, death, loss of a key loved one, childhood accidents and injuries, rape, abuse, frequent moves, moves at key times, major rejections, abandonment, car accidents, major illnesses, broken bones, losses, surgeries and invasive medical procedures, attempted suicide, near death experiences, etc.– anything that potentially had a major negative (traumatic) effect on them. Make a list if you need to.

For significantly dissociated or ritually abused survivors, the major traumatic memories are typically deeply buried or suppressed and may perhaps be irretrievable using tools you are familiar with. A tool discussed later (see step 8) has proven to be a help in this area.

Also, significantly dissociated or ritually abused survivors want to try to mentally process through the traumatic memories believing that if they understand why it happened then healing will come. This is not only *false*, but it is not part of this prayer process. The goal is to identify specific incidents from which some of the residual effects of traumatic experiences can be disconnected and removed. Any investigation or discussion of those events at this point will generally be less than productive.

2. *Disconnect from the 2nd Heaven*

This is important. Ask the Lord to disconnect them from any and all 2nd heaven entities– principalities, powers, dominions, thrones, rulers, etc. – that have gained access to them through the traumatic events they have suffered for the purpose of future torment.

I have already talked about the purposes/strategy behind the torment, but there are some terms here you may not be familiar with that might be helpful to you. What is 2nd heaven? If there's a 2nd heaven, is there a 1st, a 3rd or a 5th?

Picture it this way. We live on a big blue ball – Earth. The earth is surrounded by "atmosphere." The atmosphere is a collection of gases that are necessary to sustain life for all the people, plants, animals and bugs that live on the face of the earth, and portions of it have specific functions like absorbing the most energetic photons from the Sun, and for reflecting radio waves, thereby making long-distance radio communication possible. We know the earth's atmosphere to be approximately

450 miles in height. What is the height of the 2nd heaven? Who knows for certain, but it is inhabited by dead angelic beings which were thrown out of God's heavens in response to satan's rebellion.

The third heaven, which is above the second heaven, includes the balance of the universe, and is the dwelling place of God (see figure i.).

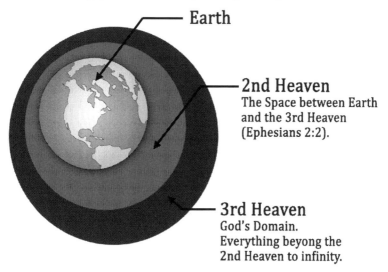

Earth

2nd Heaven
The Space between Earth and the 3rd Heaven (Ephesians 2:2).

3rd Heaven
God's Domain. Everything beyong the 2nd Heaven to infinity.

Figure i.

When satan and his dead angelic beings were cast out of heaven,[11] they wound up being given dominion over earth having deceived Adam and Eve into surrendering their dominion. Ephesians 2:2 (KJV) says, *"Wherein in time past ye walked according to the course of this world, according to the prince of the power of the air, the spirit that now worketh in the children of disobedience:"*

What we have here is lucifer (satan), as a spirit being, in a place of being able to impact (influence or control) those walking on the earth. He's no longer in God's heaven, but he also doesn't have an earth suit, so he has to hang out between the two. Father had a plan to redeem the error of man and sent us Jesus, who returned to us the original dominion of man over the earth through the authority of "the name of Jesus."

1 Corinthians 15:46 (KJV) states, *"Howbeit that was not first which is spiritual, but that which is natural; and afterward that which is spiritual."* In other words, the earthly pattern which we can discern (see and understand) with our eyes in this realm, will give us a pattern for understanding how things are structured (patterned) in the spiritual. So organizationally, what we see in the natural is generally what we can expect to see organizationally in the spiritual realm as well.

... What we see in the natural is generally what we can expect to see organizationally in the spiritual realm as well. . .

If the President of Venezuela were to decide to declare war against you, he would not fly in, catch a cab to your house, draw his sword, and pound on your door, demanding a duel in the street. No, the weasel would stand proudly on the steps of the capital building in Caracas, in full military dress uniform, the finest ceremonial sword at his side, declaring you to be the scum of the earth and that it was his sacred duty to send the army to rid the world of this dreadful menace to peace and tranquility.

When the army found its way to your neighborhood, all of his generals would not be standing at the head of the pack, but rather, the privates and the corporals. They in turn would be followed by sergeants, warrant officers, lieutenants, captains, colonels, and so on. If that's what happens in the natural, then we can expect the same thing to occur in the spiritual. You win authority in the spirit by first whipping a few privates, then a few sergeants, then a few warrant officers, etc., defeating them all in succession until the entire "dark side" capitulates and skulks off to pick on someone their own size.

Since you have proven yourself to be so tough, the president and his generals, who started the whole mess, will not come out after you.

Practically speaking, what are we dealing with here in step 2? According to Psalm 115:16 (NASB),

"The highest heavens belong to the LORD, *but the earth he has given to mankind."* From this scripture I deduce two things: a) we have been given authority over the demonic entities that touch/affect earth in the name of Jesus. Those are our responsibility; and b) the existence of principalities and powers of the 'dark side' which are the natural equivalent of generals and lt. generals, etc., that are orchestrating the attacks against your client. I consider dealing with this class of 2nd heaven entities above my pay grade, which requires that I ask the Lord himself to deal with them directly.

Where is the line between what I can deal with, and what can I ask the Lord to deal with? I wish I had a definitive answer for you. But I have learned this much: in the context of this step, I have dealt with them as a higher order of evil, such as a principality, dark power, ruler, throne or dominion, and experienced much success with breaking all their tormenting activities simply by asking God the Father to deal with them. This has been very effective in disconnecting the client from them all, whether they are demons (earth bound) or 2nd heaven entities of a higher order. It seems that the result has been all encompassing.

This step alone seems to cut off tormenting dreams for 95% of those for whom I have used this tool.

And if this is all you are able to pray due to time or opportunity, it will go a long way toward establishing freedom for them.

Use the information you learned in Step 1 to guide you in deliverance. I am finding that this is always a good strategy. You may have to lead them in a prayer to renounce agreements they made with the enemy which opened the door for demonization in several specific areas related to situations surrounding the traumatic events they suffered or that followed them. Doing so makes the deliverance go much easier on both of you.

3. Body Release
Next, tell your client what you are about to do and get their permission for you to take authority over their being/body for a few minutes to cut some things off. Begin by commanding all of the residual effects of trauma, whether it be physical, emotional or spiritual, to be released.

Each of us, whether we are familiar with it or not, store the results of traumatic events somewhere in our physical body. It would behoove you to know where you store yours. For most people, it is first noticed in the neck and shoulders, then in broader areas of the back. For some it is in the abdomen, then around the heart. It is the reason why individuals who have a massage often experience the recurrence of a memory commensurate with a painful event as the 'knots' in a specific local area of the body are worked on.

For significantly traumatic events, these "memories" are stored at the cellular level. They become chemically bonded with all manner of other chemicals present or produced in the body naturally, especially enzymes that are naturally produced by the body in response to the trauma.

Some of you reading this just got your panties all in a wad at the "all encompassing" thought of that last sentence in the first paragraph of this step. I am not uniformly declaring that everything held within the human body imparted as a result of trauma will miraculously drain out as if pulling the plug in the bathtub, nor will it evaporate as would fog burned off by morning sun. What I am saying is this: *that which will be released by your authority will be released; that which will not or cannot be released will not be released.* As much as I would like to say that someday my personal faith will rise to a place where "all things are possible" for those who have experienced severe trauma, that day probably won't happen because there is so much more in the process of restoration which is dependent solely upon the client.

Whether my clients ever achieve wholeness from the ravages of trauma is ultimately a matter that is between them and God. God is their healer, not me. There is a limit on what I can do as a priest before God on their behalf that is actually established by God. Even Jesus said (paraphrased), *"I can only do what He shows or tells me to do. Beyond that, I'm stuck just like you."*[12]

In the final analysis, healing, wholeness, restoration, however you want to refer to it, God has ordained as a process. The goal of the process is healing, wholeness, restoration for relationship, primarily with Him, but secondarily with those around them. Jesus said, *"I came that they may have life, and have it abundantly."*[13] Abundant life is not possible without fullness of relationship with Him and with others.

The extent of which the residual effects of trauma leave when I command them out of their bodies, that is the extent to which God and your client are willing to go in this process. You have no power over anything more.

Be certain to include the effects of all abuse, defiling touch, incisions, invasive medical procedures, rape, violent car accidents, major injuries, near-death experiences, rejections, abandonment, beatings/bruises, harsh words or curses spoken by parents or other significant authorities, etc. In the event of a particularly defiling activity such as rape or initial homosexual encounters, command out of their body the memory of all smells, feelings, tastes, sounds, vibrations and defiling touch connected with those events.

> ### *Jesus said, "I came that they may have life, and have it abundantly."*

I have also had success in dealing with this issue on behalf of women who discovered their husband was deep into internet pornography. There is such a deep sense of betrayal that comes along with that discovery that is so personal and shameful because it strikes at the very core of the spouse's identity and the foundation of the most intimate of relationships; therefore, it tends to be largely internalized. That response draws all manner of junk to it, which eventually finds its expression physically. Dealing with the physical effects of the trauma in this manner seems to help dial down all the remaining issues to a manageable level.

Have all parts, alters, primaries and secondaries, ego states, etc., release all memories of body and emotional trauma.

During this step I also try to make it a habit of speaking directly to their body, commanding it to release it (the residual effects of trauma), as well. Because your client will not usually be aware of what's coming next, or how this prayer process goes, you are in the driver's seat. So, do what you have to do to deal with the issues presented. You don't have to yell and scream, for neither demons, nor human cells are deaf. You either have authority or you don't. If you understand and exercise your authority, the things that need to move will move.

Require that it come out without harm or injury. Bless their lymphatic system and other systems to safely remove all wastes, toxins, poisons, or any other product or by-product of trauma from the body. Include anything that is naturally a foreign agent in the body, that was bonded to, or that the body produced in excess connected with the traumatic event.

You will notice in a moment as you progress to step four that the steps appear to be identical. What I usually prefer to do is handle all the really serious traumatic incidents first, and then I will, in a second step, handle the less serious events. Do you have to do it this way? No, it just seems to help me focus more on Holy Spirit led prayer as I move through them all and helps me not to leave anything significant out.

4. Body Release: Trauma

Take authority over their physical body and command out of it all of the long and short-term effects of trauma, injuries, stress, tension, worry, anxiety, fear, wounding, etc.

Do not hurry through this part. You will find that your client may feel things leaving them as they get progressively more relaxed. If your client has been carrying the accumulated weight of years of stress and tension, the stark contrast of the before and after will be a great surprise for them. I have had several clients actually fall asleep toward the conclusion of this section and many more unable to walk out of my office immediately afterward because they are so relaxed.

4a. Body Release: Stress

Although the experience of dealing with the stress and tension of everyday life may be difficult, it is not trauma. But, the interesting thing about dealing with the effects of trauma residing in the body is that many of the physical manifestations of the results of everyday stress, tension, and anxiety respond as though they were.

The American Psychiatric Association is a group that is very interested in how the public reacts to, and handles (or not), everyday tension, stress and anxiety. The results released of a 2010 survey seemed to indicate that most individuals consider stress to be a significant issue for them right now. Seventy-five percent of adult respondents said they had experienced moderate to high levels of stress during the previous 12 months. Women were far more likely to develop tension-induced symptoms such as lethargy, sadness, irritability and overeating.[14]

Stress triggers the release of hormones such as adrenaline and cortisol, which stimulate and prepare the body for action by accelerating heart rate, tensing major muscle groups and even thickening blood. Prolonged exposure and secretion of these enzymes produces significant health issues. Dr. Elissa Epel, psychiatry researcher at the University of California, San Francisco, states, *"We've found that over time, cortisol can wear down the protective ends of DNA. This ages the immune system, heightening a person's vulnerability to cardiovascular disease and a host of other illnesses."*[15]

Teaching your clients and/or their spouses to complete this step once a month will greatly add to their ability to stand up under stressful situations without damaging personal relationships. I have had many clients tell me they feel like they've had a massage.

4b. Body Release: Secondary Trauma

Those involved as prayer ministers and mental health care professionals specializing in the treatment of trauma hear tales of extreme human suffering and observe the emotions of fear, helplessness and horror registered by survivors on a consistent basis. Recent research demonstrates that these occupational duties may cause psychological symptoms in the practitioner who bears witness to the survivors' account of trauma.

Primary posttraumatic stress disorder (PTSD) may be diagnosed in an individual who experienced, witnessed or was confronted with a traumatic event and responded with intense fear, helplessness or horror. Intentional traumas (e.g., combat, sexual assault, SRA, terrorism and mass violence), as well as unintentional traumas (e.g., natural disasters, accidents), may also cause this condition.

Secondary trauma is defined as indirect exposure to trauma through a firsthand account or narrative of a traumatic event. The vivid recounting of trauma by the survivor and your own subsequent cognitive or emotional representation of that event may result in a set of symptoms and reactions that parallel PTSD (e.g., re-experiencing, avoidance and hyper-arousal). Secondary traumatization is also referred to as compassion fatigue and vicarious traumatization.

In the 25 years I've been praying for individuals on a part-time basis, and full-time for the last nine, I have only experienced what I would term secondary traumatization on two occasions. Both occurred following seasons of intense ministry during which I worked with five to six clients per day, one of them usually in the evening, many times six days a week. As you may be aware, working 'by the spirit' takes a significant amount of energy, which can only be replenished by spending time with God. During that period, I had let my daily time with the Lord dwindle down to 30 minutes or less, citing the heaviness of my schedule. My "immune" system was compromised.

As you may be aware, working 'by the spirit' takes a significant amount of energy, which can only be replenished by spending time with God.

The interesting thing about both experiences was that I could trace my emotional upheaval directly to a specific appointment with a client. Something about those sessions had pushed me over the limit and there was a realization that it had happened. Unfortunately, my schedule was always packed for the next 10 days, so it was usually at least that long before I could address it and make some changes, particularly if I thought I was just getting burned out.

Right after both these incidents, I couldn't just "gut it out." I felt peculiarly vulnerable, avoided people and every potentially agitating situation, became hyper-vigilant, had difficulty sleeping and became uncharacteristically fearful. Frankly, it was scary. I knew that I wasn't myself anymore, but there didn't seem to be anything I could do about it. I killed my schedule for a week and found some relief, but when I cranked it up again, there I was back in the same old place again. But even in the intervening time, I knew there was something wrong.

We are very fortunate in that, in addition to all of the personal ministry we do, we travel and teach, which breaks up the hard work. We also founded and operate the healing rooms in our local church, and have worked in them weekly for the past seven years. It was out of the strength of those relationships that I was able to get the help I needed to put my personal house back in order, and the accountability I needed to keep it there.

Our culture of independence would say, *"physician, heal thyself."*[16] If we're not careful, we can believe our own press and upon awakening one grey, overcast morning, we will gaze into the mirror and find ourselves beholding our own worst enemy who wants to pull the plug. Take personal inventory periodically. Know where you are emotionally and spiritually and don't ignore the warning signs because the enemy wants to use your compassion against you.

Most of Step 4b is dedicated to those who become traumatized through listening to the stories of those who went through horrific experiences. Still, I want to slightly expand it. Last year I prayed for a woman whose whole-hearted compassionate intercession induced a form of secondary trauma in her through attempting to help carry the burdens of others. Burden-bearing in behalf of other's suffering can be raised to an art form for some people. We must not enter into these roles lightly, but we must also guard from entering into them foolishly.

God will grant us copious amounts of grace to handle the things that happen to us, but there is no grace to handle things others are supposed to carry for themselves. Just because you feel a significant amount of compassion and feel led to pray for someone in the midst of suffering overwhelming injustice, does not mean that you automatically have the responsibility to carry it for them. Guard yourself from making more out of your own zeal to help than there is.

Secondary trauma is an interesting phenomenon that you need to pay attention to.

5. *Shut Down Enemy Pathways*

Take authority over all pathways, portals, and means of access, marks or markers, or any means of connectivity placed upon them physically or spiritually to track them or gain access to them for purposes of torment, and shut them down in the authority given to you in the name of Jesus. Ask the Lord to shut down all pathways, portals, and means of 2nd heaven access to them for communication or influence.

Cancel all assignments of familiar spirits made against them as a result of traumatic incidents, or as a result of generational trauma.

If your client has been frequently tormented by violent or sexually-oriented dreams, this (in concert with step 2 and step 4 above) will usually kill them. But, if you are uncertain or just want to cover the ground, ask the Lord to issue a "cease and desist order." If they have had violent or tormenting dreams, ask them if there is a theme or pattern to what happens to them in the dreams. Sometimes this will give you a clue as to other issues you may need to deal with in a subsequent ministry session.

On occasion, this has been an area that has been hard to get immediate and long lasting results and has caused a great deal of inquiry of the Lord and the client. A couple of times, it has been the result of the client's unconscious inner vow made during or immediately after a traumatic event. The memory of it was deeply suppressed. On a couple of other occasions, the enemy was quite creative in how a specific marker was placed and what triggered it. Just get used to thinking outside the box and allow Holy Spirit to put his finger on some of the most arcane and seemingly innocuous information.

6. Release the Prisoner

Ask the Lord that if there is any portion of their being that has been delayed, trapped, assigned, captured or imprisoned in another time, another space, another dimension or place, as a result of trauma, would He please cause it to be released and rejoined with their core being at this current time, space, dimension and maturity level. I also ask the Lord to re-unify those portions with the core person. I ask the Lord to cleanse those parts of any defilement as a result of where it has been, and to cancel the assignment of any familiar spirit connected to it.

See Isaiah 61:1-2 (KJV; emphasis added): *"The Spirit of the Lord GOD is upon me; because the LORD hath anointed me to preach good tidings unto the meek; he hath sent me to **bind up** the brokenhearted, to proclaim liberty to the **captives**, and the opening of the **prison** to them that are bound; to proclaim the acceptable year of the LORD, and **the day of vengeance of our God;** to comfort all that mourn."* (Remember that *prisoners* are there because of something they have done, whereas *captives* are imprisoned through no fault of their own.)

As Dr. Paul Cox of Aslan's Place Ministries[17] teaches, there are a couple of specific questions that you should ask of the Lord. For if the Word addresses it, we need to ask if this is an issue in this instance.

> ***Romans 8:38-39 (RSV) – "For I am persuaded, that neither death, nor life, nor angels, nor principalities, nor things present, nor things to come, nor powers, nor height, nor depth, nor any other creature, shall be able to separate us from the love of God, which is in Christ Jesus our Lord."***

Ask the Lord if there is a specific place where

portions of them have been imprisoned (e.g., anything in the passage just quoted, including Sheol). You should also ask, *"Is there anything specific to imprisonment in that place that I need to cut off?"*

If prompted by the Holy Spirit, walk them through a reunification of these fractured parts by walking them through each dimension or through each year of their lives.

In a vast majority of the occasions of praying through this process, I have the Holy Spirit prompt me to walk them slowly forward from the age of one, two or three years, year by year, until we reach their current chronological age, pausing when prompted between years to allow the Holy Spirit to re-integrate them. More recently, I have included the period from conception to birth as well when their birth mother experienced trauma herself or planned to abort the child.

I also asked Him to mature each re-integrated portion to the client's current age. Ask the Lord to move every part of them– spirit, soul, body and birthright– into the Lord's *appropriate time.* This doesn't seem to take any more time, but I believe it is worth the effort.

I also ask the Lord to release any portions of them that they intentionally dismissed from themselves because they felt it was not safe, or would be used against them. Lead them in a prayer of repentance if necessary. This is often the case for those who are moderately dissociated. When they are finished, ask if they have a picture of themselves, or if they feel any different than when they started.

If you have the time, it is appropriate for you to thoroughly deal with each of the traumatic events as they arise. This is the only manner by which permanent healing can be acquired, short of a sovereign work of the Lord.

I have not had the opportunity to use this tool in behalf of a severely abused child, or a returning Iraq war veteran, but I have no doubt that it would be equally as effective as it is with other adults, and perhaps even more so.

It is always proper (and a great idea) to coach your adult client to be aware of his/her body and report to you the changes they sense or feel as you are walking them through each year of the process. Don't get in a hurry.

I ministered to a fellow who could identify those separated parts and he said that some appeared to have been stolen from him, and some appeared to have been banished by him. The latter appears to be the result of voluntary dissociation as a result of significant stress or traumatic circumstances.

Under these conditions, you may wish to have them repent for sending these portions of them away. Ask the Lord to reunite the parts to them and refer them to someone who has knowledge and experience in dissociative issues.

I also want to say at this point that I cannot say with finality precisely what this step accomplishes. It has been markedly different with each individual. I have had some who have experienced the spontaneous re-integration of portions of their soul. I have had several who have experienced spontaneous deliverances. I have had folks who experienced nothing at the time and yet have later found themselves much more in control of their own lives. How this happens, and what actually happens, who knows. Our heavenly Father loves to orchestrate all manner of good things for people when we pray, regardless of whether we are fully aware of what is going on at the time or not. Just keep praying.

If all you have time to pray are steps 2 and 6, do it. As these are the real foundations of this tool.

7. Important Declaration

One thing I have discovered while in the midst of praying through the trauma prayer process with women who were traumatized initially as children, and re-traumatized as adults by another means (e.g., auto accident, rape, household robbery), is to direct the following powerful, yet simple "declaration" to their soul and spirit:

"You no longer have to remain on guard, in a heightened state of alertness, or remain in a state of high sensitivity to people or your surroundings. You may now rest and are supposed to enter into a natural state of rest and relaxation. The difficult event(s) is over now. You are no longer in danger. There is no longer a need to remain hyper-sensitive for the sake of personal protection or survival. Those days are over. The danger has passed. You can finally rest. Take a deep breath and exhale slowly."

Not every one of your clients will be able to respond to it. Many cannot, for it was those who were their caregivers and their trusted authorities that were usually their greatest source of abuse.

That simple suggestion, although I usually utter it as more of a direction than a suggestion, has helped a number of women begin to move from a position of being volitionally frozen, to being able to make choices once more, rapidly break long-term habits and begin to trust again.

8. Pray for the Brain

Ask the Lord to reestablish the connection between the hemispheres of the brain. Often, heavily traumatized clients live predominately out of the left hemisphere of their brain and need the right side to be stimulated. Pray that the Lord will reestablish and synchronize both explicit memory and implicit memory and reactivate any connections required to retrieve memories needed for complete healing. Pray that He would bring back into balance all chemical, electrical and magnetic communication paths within the brain and restore them to optimal levels for stability.

If prompted, I will place my hands specifically in the area near the amygdala and then the hippocampus and ask the Lord to restore them, repair them, or enhance them so that their healing can progress rapidly. There are five specific organs in the human brain that are damaged by wounding and trauma: amygdala, thalamus, hippocampus, cingulate cortex and right prefrontal cortex. These will have to be addressed later in order to assure complete healing, but pray for them individually to be fully restored if prompted.

I usually ask if I can place my hands of the head of my client while praying this section of the tool and it is usually accompanied by a strong anointing (interestingly, it is usually in my left hand only). So don't freak out if this happens to you as well.

If you are not familiar with the Thriving: Recover Your Life Program,[18] The Life Model,[19] and Equipping Hearts for Harvest,[20] you need to do so. It is all based on Dr. Jim Wilder's work in neuroscience combined with prayer ministry, as noted in his book *Life Model: Living from the Heart that Jesus Gave You.*[21] It will be something that many of those you minister to, who have been victims of severe trauma, will need to help them rebuild their lives. According to their understanding, these are some specific wounds that heavily impact a specific element of the brain:

Thrive Program Foundational Elements

Level	Thrive Principle	Type of Pain	Answer	Brain
1	A place to Belong	A painful existence, not knowing who and what is personal to me.	Two Bonds for life. Brains can have high capacity for complex emotions.	Attachment Center (Thalmus)
2	Receiving and Giving Life (engage or avoid)	Fearful Reality	A Helper with a fearless brain.	Engage vs. Avoid (amygdale)
3	Trauma Recovery of Emotions	Continuing emotional distress and unregulated energy levels.	Trained brain – able to return to joy from 6 emotions.	Management Distressing Energy (Cingulate)
4	Maturity	Loss of focus and reactivity. Immaturity and an under-developed sense of morality	Community	Joy Center Focused Attention/Maturity (right prefrontal cortex)
5	Cohesive Identity (living from the heart)	Lack of cohesive identity. Right and Left hemispheres of the brain de-synchronized. Internal Conflict	Internal resolution through spiritual intervention	Coherent Identity (left hemisphere). Hearing from God

Figure ii.

These individual programs will also be helpful in aiding those of your clients who have suffered extensively and should be part of any structured resocialization process. These programs, individually and collectively, will help clients recover their lives because each of these 12 week programs are conducted within the context of small groups. Small group participation with those who have also suffered much is a key to opening the doors of trust once again. These programs are an integral part of every healing community I am aware of which successfully ministers to those who have been severely traumatized and abused.

9. Destroy Secular Structures
In the name of Jesus, tear down all existing structure of understanding and thought established according to the world's system. These are the mental ideologies, understandings and structures of thoughts taught to us by our ancestors and our immediate family about why things are the way they are (called their truth) and why we should be afraid of them or treat them in a certain fashion. In time, they become your truth, even if it has no resemblance to the real truth and reality of life at all. These are often identified as the family prides and prejudices inherent in a family's line, including such things as misogyny, misandry, denial, poverty, rebellion, isolation, etc.

In the name of Jesus, ask God to establish His Kingdom concepts, structures, principles and understandings over the individual and his/her family line.

10. *Restoring Sleep Patterns*

Ask the Lord to reestablish for them the appropriate sleep patterns the Lord designed for them and to establish for them a sweet, undisturbed, rejuvenating, regenerative rest.

Proverbs 3:24 (NASB) – *"When you lie down, you will not be afraid; when you lie down, your sleep will be sweet."*

Ask the Lord to begin or reestablish Godly dreams, visions and angelic visitations in the night seasons, both to enlighten, instruct and direct them.

Job 33:15-16 (NKJV) – *"In a dream, in a vision of the night, when deep sleep falls upon men, in slumbering upon the bed; then he opens men's ears, and seals their instruction."*

Psalm 4:8 (ASV) – *"In peace will I both lay me down and sleep; For thou, Jehovah, alone makest me dwell in safety."*

I have had numerous clients report that following the ministry session, they fell asleep immediately, stayed asleep, and were not awakened by tormenting dreams the entire night for the first time in years. The immediate restoration of sleep patterns happens for almost the entirety of my clients but a reestablishment of Godly dreams for only about 70% initially. I believe this is a function of the reestablishment of sound sleep which has usually been deprived for years.

Sleep deprivation is one of the major tactics the enemy uses to destroy physical and emotional health.

11. *Dismantle the Pushbuttons*

Ask the Lord to begin to dismantle all automatic human responses gained as a result of trauma, e.g., abnormal fright responses, triggers, fears and phobias. Pray over their brain for the Lord to rebuild, reestablish, and recreate any electrical or chemical connections broken or improperly re-connected as a result of trauma so that the individual can operate once again within normal limits of high and low stimulus, and can remain in control emotionally when the stimulus exceeds those limits.

This will also be key to pray over anyone who has experienced significant physical abuse, a traumatic brain injury, a major auto accident, and so on.

I try to make it common practice to ask the Lord to dismantle any emotional pushbuttons or triggers the enemy has installed as a result of trauma, especially those that are triggered by sights, sounds, smells or feelings. We do not want a client to be unnecessarily triggered by extraneous outside stimulus, but we do want them to maintain or regain access to memories needful for complete healing. So I ask the Lord to re-orient the filing cabinet of memories, making the ugly ones harder to get to and yet still accessible, while moving the good memories, those that speak to them of value, purpose, belonging and love, to a place where they are the first ones they go to.

I have had numerous clients report that following the ministry session they no longer have most (or all) of their long-term, exaggerated fright responses. This is certainly not universal, but is a relatively common experience.

All of us are programmed with an innate fight or flight response. It is part of our normal survival mode of operation. If the experience does not have a frightful component to it, the fight or flight response is not triggered. If the situation does engender sudden fear in the individual, there is a decision inherent in the normal process that cause us to determine which of those avenues provides us the best choice of survival. Those who have an exaggerated fright response never get to the decision point of choosing whether to fight or flee; they are frozen in fright. Once there, everything in the world that startles them (or comes even slightly unexpectedly), is seen as a serious threat and they are once again frozen in their own fear. If the fright response is never dealt with, they can become reclusive and prisoners in their own home. Unfortunately, once the door to fear is opened, it is unrelenting. They do not deem their own familiar home any safer than being elsewhere unprotected.

They also frequently report that there seems to be a level of peace that they can rest in that they've not had before. They can actually sit before the Lord without their mind racing to things they have to do, issues that must resolve, or losses they are about to incur. They report that the internal wars and conflict, fears and insecurities, and the eternal unanswered questions are still buzzing around in there, but it is wonderful in comparison to what it used to be.

12. Reestablish Appropriate Time

One of the interesting things about life is time and our association with it. Psalm 115:16 (BBE) says, *"The heavens, are the LORD'S; but the earth He has given to the children of men."* That verse establishes a couple of things for us:

1. Time only affects the earth and our relationship to the balance of the universe, principally

because of the aging process, finite life span, and our strictly linear view of things in general;

2. Since God exists outside of time, He can be in the future, past or present at the same time;

3. Since time only affects earth, we as the children of men have been given authority over time.

Ecclesiastes 3:1-8 (NKJV):

"To everything there is a season, and a time to every purpose under the heaven: a time to be born, and a time to die; a time to plant, and a time to pluck up that which is planted; a time to kill, and a time to heal; a time to break down, and a time to build up; a time to weep, and a time to laugh; a time to mourn, and a time to dance;

"A time to cast away stones, and a time to gather stones together; a time to embrace, and a time to refrain from embracing; a time to seek, and a time to lose; a time to keep, and a time to cast away; a time to rend, and a time to sew; a time to keep silence, and a time to speak; a time to love, and a time to hate; a time for war, and a time for peace."

Abnormalities in time can either be natural or spiritual, but the result is usually the same.

If a client's childhood was terrible, they may want to live in the future where they believe that things will be better for them. If a client's present circumstances are horrible, they may want to live in the future where they believe that they will live a more preferable lifestyle, or in the past when things were actually better. In any event, the client is not living in the present. The present is the only place where problems can be addressed and solved; the past is gone and the future is not yet here; a double bind of significant proportions.

Another way people are stuck in time is through significant wounds as children, or a sudden untimely loss (particularly of a loved one) through which the remainder of life has been defined.

I ministered to a woman in her 70's whose childhood was one filled with physical and mental abuse. Her mother was a life-long alcoholic and was in bed half the time. As the oldest, she was her sibling's caretaker from a very young age. Her level of wounding was significant enough that as a child she had considered taking her life to escape it. As an adult she felt trapped by the wounds, the results of the wounding, and an inability to conduct relationships on a normal level because she didn't know what normal was. She had always felt that she had never been prepared for real life because of the childhood wounds and dysfunctional upbringing. As her own children grew into their 30's, she became increasingly remorseful that she had not done a proper job raising her children because of her screwed up family history. She was trapped in the past.

In a very real sense she was bound to the past by her own assumptions of how poorly she had raised her own children and conducted personal relationships throughout the years. She was also blocked from accepting herself and a more acceptable future by her assumption that she could never move forward because her mother had never prepared her to do so.

Another explanation for suffering abnormalities in time is through a significant tragedy or traumatic event, particularly experienced as a child, as a result of which a portion of their development becomes arrested, i.e., stuck in time.

For those who are not living in the present, in order for healing and restoration to begin, the client must make a choice to live in the present. In order for that to happen, your client must repent for choosing to live elsewhere and begin to live in the present. This must be done by a verbal declaration on their part.[22]

This does not mean they have to live in denial about how ugly things were or are currently. It *does* mean that they have to choose to not allow the past to define their future. In other words, they must come out from under the mindset of the world. The world's system wants to determine your qualifications for success and thusly, pre-set your personal expectations of achievement. If you had a bad childhood, full of disappointment and devastation, that automatically disqualifies you for receiving favor and reward. If both your parents were ignorant, alcoholic, welfare recipients, then certainly the highest you can climb from the ditch you were raised in is to be an educated, non-alcoholic, welfare recipient. Our God is redemptive in all his ways, automatically means that your past – however disqualifying it may be – does not dictate your future because you can do all things through Christ.

How do you do it?

First of all, you have to deal with what caused it. The will of the individual was engaged in a cause-and-effect, action-reaction situation. They made a decision that put them in this place. They have to repent (i.e., make a different decision) to get out of that place. Lead them in a repeat-after-me prayer that has them renounce making the original decision. Then lead them to declare what they will do in the future (i.e., live in the present).

Have them renounce their agreement with the system of this world. Have them ask forgiveness of the Father for choosing to live basing their expectations of what He would/could do for them upon their current circumstances.

Have them repent for choosing to live life according to the dictates of the past.

Our God is redemptive in all his ways, automatically means that your past – however disqualifying it may be – does not dictate your future because you can do all things through Christ.

According to Psalm 115:16, we have the authority to reset time for them. Just command it in the name of Jesus. If that's not your style, ask the Lord to do it for them by a prayer inviting the Lord to restore them to their proper place in time and cleanse the time of any defilement initiated by their sin.

As a fellow steward of the earth, you can give the Lord permission to enter into the affairs of men to be redemptive. Simply ask him to reset the individual's internal time, and the time of all alters and fractures, to the current time – to the current place, domain and space. If the term domain is troublesome for you, hang on, we'll get there. This will assist in helping establish them in a place where they can begin to not only make better decisions, but make them independently (or on their own).

For girls coming out of the sex trade who are in their late teens or early twenties, they usually entered it around 12 to 13 years of age, some younger. That activity awakened their sexual capacity, capability, thoughts, and expression long before the appropriate chronological time. The same is true for young men who were exposed to pornography. Ask the Lord to restore the defiled portion of them to that pre-awakened state, emotionally and physically. Ask Him to remove all defilement of time, defilement of place, domain and space from them physically, emotionally and spiritually.

I also ask the Lord to unify all their systems to their current chronological age and maturity level, operating as it would if nothing had been awakened out of time and season.

Like any other ministry activity, don't pray or minister with your eyes closed. Many people have been so shut down that you need to be aware of any change that is demonstrated during a session – changes such as eye twitches, hand/finger movements, sounds, shift of body position, tension, breathing rate, not to mention smells or any other experience which is not "normal." These reactions will give you clues for where to head next in ministry session(s).

At this point, I usually move right into some form of the Trauma Prayer Process noted elsewhere in this manual. I may have them break agreement with any spirit they contracted within the process of the awakening and any actions of their own which ratified those agreements.

On numerous occasions your clients will have some sort of physical reaction to the process. Have them describe what they are feeling or sensing as you walk through this process. If anything significant occurs, pursue it at the Lord's direction.

13. Connect with God

Then instruct the client to instruct (tell or direct) his/her human spirit each evening before going to sleep, to turn its face to the Father during the night while the body and soul are out cold, and receive everything he/she needs for the coming day.

Psalm 16:7 (ASV) – *"I will bless Jehovah, who hath given me counsel; Yea, my heart instructeth me in the night seasons."*

You and I are made in the image of God. *He never sleeps nor slumbers.*[23] It's my guess that your spirit doesn't either. So why not put it to work? I think that's what David did.

It is my belief that David fully understood his need for wisdom and understanding in ruling over Israel, which to my mind is why his son, Solomon, responded to God as he did. In response to God's question in 1 Kings 3:7-9, Solomon replied that he needed understanding and discernment. God knows who we're going to bump into tomorrow, what crisis we'll face, what wisdom we'll need, what counsel we'll be called on to provide. Why not ask him to load you up with whatever you need for the coming day while you're laying around doing nothing?

14. Personal Blessing

I usually close each session with some kind of a blessing. So many people we minister to have never had a real blessing and long to have one. You can write it out and read it to them if you wish, or you and Holy Spirit can wing it. Those are the most fun because you can look them in the eye when you do it. It seems to carry so much more weight with them because eye to eye contact is both intimate and maximizes communication.

Note: In recent days I have come to the conclusion that if this prayer process is to have maximum benefit, it should be prayed over an individual three (3) times. Things typically come off in layers; so it is with this issue.

For two weeks I have noticed a little girl drawing monsters at our House of Prayer. I asked her, "do you see them a lot?"

"Yes," she said.

"Are you afraid?"

" Yes."

"Do you want them to go away?"

"Yes."

I asked Jesus to remove all effects of trauma over her - body soul and spirit. Startled, she opened her eyes. I asked what happened.

She said, "They went away!"

Praise you Jesus!

Ministering Over Trauma in Children

Chapter written by Pat Banks

The tools for ministering to children who have suffered trauma are much the same as you would use for an adult. The application of those tools, however, will be significantly different.

Several factors have to be taken into consideration before beginning ministry to a child:

1. Age
2. Type of trauma
3. Parental involvement in the trauma
4. Caretakers
5. Spiritual background

When a child experiences a trauma before the age of cognitive reasoning ability, they experience pain

.nd confusion without the ability to properly assess truth. Because there is within everyone a sense of right and wrong, the young one may know that what has happened is bad but their ability to determine their part in it is very limited, which usually results in misinterpretation. God made children to expect unconditional love from those who are supposed to take care of them. If a family member is the cause of the trauma, the child will, more often than not, blame themselves for it.

Once the child believes that it was their fault, shame, guilt, self-hatred, performance (trying to please the perpetrator), or even the belief that the behavior which caused the trauma is normal, may result. The child, however, has no mechanism in them to deal with the pain incurred.

Since the trauma prayer ministry is not counseling, it is possible to deal with the spirit of the child without them having to be in a position to comprehensively understand the issue. At an early age, the goal is to keep the lies the enemy will feed them from taking root in their spirit and soul. Even though we cannot remove the memory of the event from their minds, we can deal with the spiritual attack from the enemy launched against them by the trauma by effectively dealing with all the ungodly beliefs (lies).

There is a very basic belief which must be held by the prayer minister before they will be accepting of this method. That belief is that children can suffer spiritual attack even though they do not understand what is happening to them. These attacks can set in motion a belief structure which will affect the rest of the child's life. The traumatic incident could be seemingly small to adult minds or extremely horrific. The issue is not how the adult thinks it should have affected the child, but how the child processed it.

At an early age, the goal is to keep the lies the enemy will feed them from taking root in their spirit and soul.

In order to keep from trying to analyze the child, the prayer minister can use the tool and adjust it to the issues which the Holy Spirit would highlight for each child.

In cases of younger children, from birth to age 9 or 10, depending upon the maturity level of the child, the prayer minister simply exercises his/her authority over the effects of trauma, generational sin, physical wounding or other items which may be involved, similar to the manner in which we deal with trauma in adults

In praying for the little ones, it is best to have a safe adult let the child sit in their lap or let the child play while being prayed for. The child's attention is not necessary to deal with the spiritual aspects of trauma.

A safe and familiar environment is best. The method of prayer should be gentle when the child is present. No screaming or yelling; *the enemy responds to authority, not volume.* Let's not traumatize them further by our prayers.

Repentance Prayers

When a child reaches an age where they understand that they have agreed and participated in things that were wrong, you can lead them in some very simple 'repeat after me' repentance prayers. This will help them understand that repentance is not a hard or bad thing as well as set their will toward wholeness.

We must not forget that a child has a sin nature which naturally gravitates toward the enemy and his lies. So even though they may be a true victim, we want to make sure they know there is a way out of their pain through Jesus.

Prayer Ministry

If the child seems to feel safe and comfortable, it might be well to see if they are able to engage with Jesus, hear his voice, or see him in a safe place with them, not at the place of trauma. If the child can begin to interact with Jesus in a safe place, they will have a way to deal with future pain and lies. Sozo[24] for children is an excellent tool for teaching children how to do this, as well as application of the Immanuel Method.[25]

If the child is not able to connect with Jesus, make sure they understand they haven't done anything wrong and Jesus isn't mad at them. Remember, many children have no concept of the True Jesus and may certainly have never been introduced to this concept of interacting with Him in this way.

The following trauma prayer was used at a children's home with children ages 1 to 13. The ideal scenario is for someone to pray against the effects of trauma three times or more over the child. This is because it goes to different levels and the Holy Spirit may show other areas of attachment as you pray.

You will notice that in the prayer, we deal with generational issues that may be in operation over the child. This removes the legal right the enemy may have to torment the child. The Word says we have the power to forgive sin.[26] This is not a salvation issue for the child, but an effort to restore freedom to the child to make right choices, prayerfully making it easier for the child to come to salvation and the goodness of God.

Because we believe trauma is a door to demonic entities, it is important to disconnect the child from anything which may have gained access to them through the experience of trauma. The rest of the prayer is fairly self-explanatory.

Trauma Prayer

(Where there are blanks, insert the name of the person being prayed over)

"Father, I thank you that you have given us the authority on earth to forgive sin because of the shed blood of Jesus Christ. So in His name I forgive the sins of _____'s ancestors who opened the door to any sins, iniquitous stronghold of thought, or curses to be passed down the family line. I tear down any demonic belief structures that have been erected from the tree of the knowledge of good and evil. I cut them free from all lies they have been told or have believed about themselves.

"I ask you, Father, to disconnect _____ from any second heaven entity that has gained access to _____ as a result of the things they have suffered, specifically from any entity associated with trauma.

"I ask you, Father, to release any part of them that has been stuck or frozen in some other time, space or dimension as a result of any trauma they may have experienced. I ask you to remove all defilement, fear, or torment from that part and allow it to reintegrate to its proper place and maturity level.

"I ask you to begin this process even in the womb and move through the years of their life.

"I command all trauma and its results to leave this body now, in the name of Jesus. I command any chemicals, drugs, sights, smells or sounds that are still influencing _____ to be released right now in Jesus' name. I speak peace to every part of this body, mind and spirit.

"I command the brain cells and neurons to fire properly and make original design connections.

"I command the right and left hemispheres of the brain to work together in perfect harmony.

"I ask you, Father, to restore proper sleep patterns in _____and Holy Spirit I ask you to fill every place where trauma or its effects have left.

"Father, I call _____'s spirit to attention and I speak to _____'s spirit to remember the Father and the plan the Father has for _____."

Declaration of Worth

Then pronounce a declaration of worth, value and acceptance from the Father. Make sure you aim it toward their identity as the Father's child, not in accordance with their ability to perform and be obedient.

Remember, children don't have to mentally understand what you are declaring and praying because their spirit will. If you can get them to engage eye to eye, it would be great.

You will note that the last thing done in the prayer is to minister to the spirit of the child. This is an intentional speaking to the place where the identity of the child is formed, which trauma was aimed at damaging. This is when you will speak a blessing of true identity into the spirit of the child, building up the spirit of the child to be nurtured so as to be able to heal the soul and allow the child to walk in their true identity. This part would most beneficially be done over and over by those who are in authority over the child. This develops a platform of truth for the child's life to be built on.

I just wanted to let you know that two nights ago, I started playing the Trauma Prayer for the [my] girls. First "A" listened to it while I tucked her in. I didn't tell her much about it, just that it was a nice prayer to relieve stress. Right after it started, she was feeling things in the spirit and describing them to me (without my asking or giving her any clue that things in the spirit would be happening); such as in the beginning, when Jim "clears the air" she described something tighten in her chest, and then leave her. During the prayer, she said "I feel something velvety going down my throat, I'm drinking this nice, velvety stuff and it feels so good." Wow.

Next I placed my laptop in "H's" room while she was sleeping and it played all night in her room, over and over. In the morning she asked who that nice man was and I told him who he was and that it was a nice prayer to relieve stress. [The day was extremely busy]. Suddenly I realized she had not had a single melt down all day and that she had been so calm and sweet. Also, she had not been hyper and or aggressive toward anyone. So I brought up the subject and asked how she had felt during the day. She smiled and said, "I did not feel so jumpy today." I asked if she thought that prayer by that nice man helped and she said "yeah, he made me feel so good." She then asked if she could listen to it all night last night again, which I did. I am amazed at how CALM she is! Could this be "goodbye" to her anxiety?

God is so amazing! Just thought I'd share!

Trauma Prayer for Victims of Trafficking

Chapter written by Becca Wineka

Through a brief interview, ask the person receiving ministry to recall trauma that they incurred in childhood through their present age (they can be general and do not need to be name specific). Despite the fact that this prayer process does not require any significant amount of interaction, you will need some sort of information to work with. If giving you a significant amount of history is too difficult for them the first time this prayer is administered, ask if they can give you four or five key words that vaguely describe the situation(s) without going into detail, such as beating, rape, etc. They may be more open the second or third ministry session. It is important that you ask the person receiving ministry for their permission to take authority over their body and to begin praying things off of them. Instruct them to close their eyes and relax, reporting anything to you as it changes (feelings, thoughts, impressions, etc.). Be sure to inquire from time to time if they are quiet.

Then, begin with some equivalent to the trauma prayer below:

(Where there are blanks, insert the name of the person being prayed over)

"Father, I thank you that you have given us the authority as the sons of God to forgive sins on earth through the shed blood of Jesus Christ. In Jesus' name, I forgive the sins of _____ and the sins of their entire generational line back to Adam to the present for anything relative to prostitution. I ask You, Father, to apply the blood of Your Son, Jesus, to _____ and their family line, cleansing them from all unrighteousness and breaking all curses and consequences of iniquity and sin. Father, will you begin to send for the blessings of _____'s family line, cleansed from all iniquity and defilement?"

(Ask them to "repeat after me," if they can.)

"Father God, in Jesus' name, I break any and all soul ties with all sexual partners and

command that all parts of them be returned back to them cleansed by the Blood of Jesus; and I call back all parts of myself from them cleansed from all defilement through the Blood of Jesus. Father, I thank you for completely severing me from these soul ties."

"Father, in the name of Jesus, I ask that you would disconnect _____ from any and all second heaven entities that have gained access to _____ through the traumatic events they have experienced for the purposes of future torment."

(You can go back to anything they mentioned in the interview before prayer and name them.)

"In Jesus' name, I command all of the residual effects of trauma – physical, mental, emotional, spiritual, and sexual – be released out of _____ and go to the feet of Jesus without harm or injury. I take authority over the effects of all abuse, defiling touch, incisions, invasive medical procedures, all manner of abuse, rape, violent car accidents, major injuries, near-death experiences, rejections, abandonment, beatings/bruises, harsh or threatening words, or curses spoken by pimps, John's[27], parents, lovers, etc., and command them to be released out of _____ and go to Jesus.

"In Jesus' name, I command out of _____'s body the memory of all smells, feelings, tastes, sounds, vibrations and defiling touch connected with any rape, sexual relationship, or any homosexual relationships. In Jesus' name, I bless _____'s lymphatic system and other systems to safely remove all wastes, drugs, toxins, poisons, and chemicals, and their effects from the body."

(Speak directly to the person's body at this point.)

"In Jesus' name, I take authority over _____'s physical body and command out of it all the long and short-term effects of trauma, injuries, stress, tension, worry, anxiety, fear, torment, wounding, etc.

"In Jesus' name, I take authority over all pathways, portals, and means of access, marks or markers, or any means of connectivity placed upon _____, physically or spiritually, to track them or gain access to them for purposes of torment (future and present), and I shut them down in the Name of Jesus Christ."

"Father, will You shut down all pathways, portals, and means of second heaven access to them for communication or influence? In Jesus' name, I cancel all assignments of familiar spirits made against _____ as a result of traumatic incidents, or as a result of generational trauma.

"I ask You, Father, to release any part of them that has been trapped in any time, space, or dimension in the universe as a result of any trauma they have experienced. I ask you to remove all defilement, fear, and/or torment from that part and allow it to reintegrate to its proper place and maturity of _____'s present age. Lord, I ask that You would begin to re-unify those portions with _____'s core person and cancel the assignment of any familiar spirit connected to it. Father, I ask you to begin this process even in the womb and proceed to the current age."

(Listen and move slowly year to year to listen for what Holy Spirit wants to do. Do not be in a hurry.)

"Father, I ask that you would reestablish the connection between the left and right hemispheres of the brain bringing all chemicals, synapses, firings, and memories into balance and healing. Lord, will You rebuild, reestablish, re-create any electrical or chemical any connections broken or improperly re-connected, as a result of trauma so that _____ can operate once again within normal limits of high and low stimulus, and can remain in control emotionally when the stimulus exceeds those limits?

"I ask you, Father, to reestablish the appropriate sleep pattern that You have designed for _____ and bring them into Your sweet sleep that restores, regenerates, and renews the spirit, soul, and body.

"Father, in Jesus' name, will You begin to dismantle all automatic human responses gained as a result of trauma such as abnormal fright responses, triggers, fears and phobias that are triggered by sights, sounds, smells, feelings, or touch? Lord, would you begin bringing all things under Your control and into Your love, allowing _____ to enter into Your rest – spirit, soul, and body?"

Bless their spirit as the Lord fills you and leads you. Try to make eye contact with them if possible. If not, it is alright, as their spirit will respond with or without it.

I have been using a program called Counsel/TXP from the American Association of Christian Counselors for about a year now. One of the assessments that I use measures the client's sense of distress, anxiety, depression and personal safety. It prints out a bar graph that scores the assessment.

I have been praying your Trauma Prayer Process over my church, my friends and anyone I could find that were victims of trauma. This past Tuesday, I combined the two resources together for the first time. When my client came in, I gave him the test. He scored in the extreme elevation to dangerously elevated ranges, right at 138 and 139 (max score for this test is 140). This is the third time I have seen the 19 year-old young man. The first time I saw him he had holes in his arms where his mother had beaten him repeatedly with a 2x4, with a nail in it. I felt impressed to pray the Trauma Prayer Process over him. During the prayer, he fell asleep. After prayer, he said that he felt different, that a peace had settled down on him.

I wondered if that peace was measurable on the assessment. I then gave him the test again, and when it was scored, the reductions were amazing. Every score was in the average range. His entire test had been reduced by three standard deviations! The young man left feeling better than he had for over 5 years.

Thank you for the Trauma Prayer. Jesus is in it!"

Ministering to the Homeless

Chapter written by Becca Wineka

Homelessness is not a respecter of persons. The population of homeless in the U.S. ranges from children to the elderly. There are many variables in establishing national estimates as to the number of persons living among us who are homeless. The National Law Center on Homelessness and Poverty states that approximately 3.5 million people (1.35 million of them children) are likely to experience homelessness in a given year (2007 report). Beyond the statistics are the faces and names of the many that need to encounter the love of Jesus in their often traumatized lives.[28]

There are many reasons that a person may have found themselves facing homelessness. Some of the reasons revolve around the inability to become a functioning adult, able to responsibly maintain a day to day life. For others it may be a matter of having many problems all at once that comes caving in on them due to job loss, natural disasters, or poverty. Other reasons which revolve around relationships include: the inability for interpersonal relationships, the loss of loved ones, domestic violence, divorce and family dispute. Some people facing homelessness are battling mental/emotional issues such as depression, post-traumatic stress disorder, untreated mental illness, and physical disabilities. War veterans represent one-fifth to one-fourth of the entire homeless population nationwide.[29]

The National Law Center on Homelessness and Poverty states that approximately 3.5 million people (1.35 million of them children) are likely to experience homelessness in a given year

One of the biggest issues facing the homeless is violence. They are often left wide open to attack simply because they are uncovered and unprotected by the four walls of a house. Often times, they can be found under overpasses, out in the woods, in alley ways, and in parks, left open to the elements and to perpetrators. Since many of them are not connected with family and their whereabouts unknown, they become an easy target for "thrill-seekers" and others who have ulterior motives but are seeking prey.

Many homeless, regardless of gender, face the trauma of physical abuse and rape, sometimes by gangs. The harsh reality for the homeless often boils down to survival. This is one of the areas in which men physically overpower a woman from sheer strength. A majority of homeless women are victims of domestic violence. Many sustain injuries including broken bones, bruising, stabbings, shootings, threats, and emotional manipulation and control.

Substance and tobacco use are common practices among the homeless. The accompanying addictions of such use compounds their inability to function responsibly as an adult, spouse, employee, etc. Roughly 38% of homeless people are dependent on alcohol and 26% abuse drugs. Some will prostitute themselves to get an addiction 'fix' as well.[30]

A common spiritual reality among the homeless is the presence of the demonic in operation. Many are driven into isolation and loneliness, which has serious implications on the human spirit, soul, and body. This is especially true for the homeless. With approximately 20-25% experiencing mental illness, these souls are like open houses for the devil's minions.

The lack of hygienic care caused by adverse living conditions causes many to face physical problems such as respiratory infections, skin diseases, or exposure to tuberculosis or HIV. Physical needs often go unmet due to improper health care or neglect. Physical disabilities are common among the homeless.

God encouraged us (Becca & Kristine) to take a homeless woman into our home in the summer of 2009, after encountering her at a local grocery store parking lot. It was both an informative and unforgettable three week adventure loving on a woman who was tucked inside the heart of Father God.

In Matthew 25:35 (NASB) Jesus says, *"For I was hungry, and you gave Me something to eat; I was thirsty, and you gave Me something to drink; I was a stranger, and you invited Me in."* The homeless are on His heart and the invitation to His banquet has gone out to those who are traveling on the highways and byways of this world.[31] It is our call to compel them to come in. For us, it was a three week season to have our hearts touched for a 'stranger' and to feel His love for her and others like her.

Note: Feel free to use the following prayer in any way you choose, allowing the Holy Spirit to re-form it or add to it as you become comfortable with it. The ideal is simply to become so familiar with the main points to be covered that you allow the Holy Spirit to pray the whole thing through you over the individual, allowing for your own spiritual gifting to be expressed in the context of the session. It is not even necessary to cover each point as much as it is to pray what you feel the heart of God is for the one before you.

Sample Trauma Prayer for the Homeless

Through a brief interview, ask the person receiving ministry to recall trauma that they incurred in childhood through their present age (they can be general and do not need to be name specific). Things can be lumped together, as it is not important to have specific, detailed accounts (beatings, abuse, rapes], etc), but you do need some information in order to assess the degree of trauma you are dealing with. It also helps you connect and build trust with them. It is important to ask the person in ministry for their permission to take authority over their body and to begin praying things off of them. Instruct them to close their eyes and relax, reporting anything to you as it changes (feelings, thoughts, impressions, etc.). Be sure to inquire as to how they are doing from time to time, if they are quiet.

(Where there are blanks, insert the name of the person being prayed over)

"Father, I thank you that you have given us the authority as the sons of God to forgive sins on earth through the shed blood of Jesus Christ. In Jesus' name, I forgive the sins of _____ and the sins of their entire generational line back to Adam to the present for the sins of addiction, alignment with demons, lies, poverty mindsets, hopelessness, despair, and depression. I ask You, Father, to apply the blood of Your Son, Jesus, to _____ and their family line, cleansing them from all their sin and iniquity relative to homelessness, destruction, and chaos.

"Father, will You cancel the assignments of all familiar generational spirits, all roaming and nomadic spirits, and associated spirits that have gained access through agreements made with isolation, loneliness, depression and despair? Father, cleanse _____ from all this unrighteousness and break all curses and consequences of such iniquity and sin. Father, will you begin to send the blessings of _____'s family line, cleansed from all iniquity and defilement?

(Ask them to "repeat after me" if they can, especially with cases of domestic violence.)

"Father, in Jesus' name, I break any and all soul ties with all sexual partners and command that all parts of them be returned back to them cleansed by the Blood of Jesus; and I call back all parts of myself from them cleansed from all defilement through the Blood of Jesus. Father God, thank you for completely severing me from these soul ties."

"Father, in the name of Jesus, I ask that you would disconnect _____ from any and all second heaven entities that have gained access to _____ through the traumatic events they have experienced for the purposes of future torment.

(You can go back to anything they mentioned in the interview before prayer and name them.)

"In Jesus' name, I command all of the residual effects of trauma– physical, mental, emotional, spiritual, and sexual – to be released out of _____ and go to the feet of Jesus without harm or injury. I take authority over the effects of all abuse, defiling touch, incisions, invasive medical procedures, all manner of abuse, rape, violent car accidents, major injuries, near-death experiences, rejections, abandonment, beatings/bruises, exposure to the elements, harsh or threatening words, or curses spoken by perpetrators, parents, lovers, those in shelters, etc., and command it to be released out of _____ and go to the feet of Jesus.

"In Jesus' name, I command out of _____'s body the memory of all smells, feelings, tastes, sounds, vibrations and defiling touch connected with any rape, sexual relationship, assault or any homosexual relationships. In Jesus' name, I bless _____'s lymphatic system and other systems to safely remove all wastes, drugs, toxins, poisons, chemicals, and their effects from the body.

(Speak directly to the person's body at this point.)

"In Jesus' name, I take over _____'s physical body and command out of it all the long and short-term effects of trauma, injuries, stress, tension, worry, anxiety, fear, torment, wounding, etc.

"In Jesus' name, I take authority over all pathways, portals, and means of access, marks or markers, or any means of connectivity placed upon _____, physically or spiritually, to track them or gain access to them for purposes of torment (future and present), and I shut them down in the name of Jesus Christ."

"Father, will You shut down all pathways, portals, and means of second heaven access to them for communication or influence? In Jesus' name, I cancel all assignments of familiar spirits made against _____ as a result of traumatic incidents, assaults, or as a result of generational trauma and poverty.

"I ask You, Father, to begin releasing any part of them that has been trapped in any time, space, or dimension in the universe as a result of any trauma they have experienced. I ask you to remove all defilement, fear, and/or torment from that part and allow it to reintegrate to its proper place and maturity of _____'s present age. Lord, I ask that You would begin to re-unify those portions with _____'s core person and cancel the assignment of any familiar spirit connected to it. Father, I ask you to begin this process even in the womb and proceed to the current age.

(Listen and move slowly year to year to listen for what Holy Spirit wants to do. Do not be in a hurry.)

"Father, I ask that you would reestablish the appropriate connections between the left and right hemispheres of the brain bringing all chemicals, synapses, firings and memories into balance and healing. Lord, will You rebuild, reestablish, re-create any electrical or chemical connections broken or improperly reconnected, as a result of trauma so that _____ can operate once again within normal limits of high and low stimulus, and can remain in control emotionally when the stimulus exceeds those limits (see the chapter, "Freedom from Trauma" for specific parts of the brain)?

"I ask you, Father, to reestablish the appropriate sleep pattern that You have designed for _____ and bring them into Your sweet sleep that restores, regenerates, and renews the spirit, soul, and body.

"Father, in Jesus' name, will You begin to dismantle all automatic human responses gained as a result of trauma, poverty, and isolation such as abnormal fright responses, triggers, fears and phobias that are triggered by sights, sounds, smells, feelings, or touch? Lord, would you begin bringing all things under Your control and into Your love, allowing _____ to enter into Your rest– spirit, soul, and body?

"Father, in Jesus' name, would You begin to fill all vacancies in this house with the healing light of Your presence, with perfect peace, filling all spaces and voids where the enemy has left? I ask that Your mind, Jesus, is present in them as Your child and that You would flood their hearts with Your joy and resurrection life. Thank you, Father, for Your banner of love over _____'s life, relationships, and the path of righteousness where the light of Your lamp leads them. Thank you for making all of the crooked places straight and level and for leading _____ in Your truth and into the destiny that You have for _____."

Bless their spirit as the Lord fills you and leads you. Try to make eye contact with them if possible. If not, their spirit will respond with or without it.

I just wanted to let you know how amazing the Trauma prayer has been! I sent out about 20 copies of the prayer and so far have received about 7 testimonies of how people were miraculously healed or had sleeping problems and can now sleep!

One lady said that before getting the CD and listening to it she had to go to the emergency room because she had been unable to sleep for several nights. They gave her medication but since listening to the CD, she no longer has to take the medication.

Another friend's husband has been very sick for years and had just got out of the hospital after another surgery and was still very sick but since listening to the CD, he now feels fine!

Someone even played it at the church I used to go to with great results!

God is so good. I just love the way he orchestrates things.

Ministering to Victims of Trauma in Prisons and Residential Drug Rehab Centers

Chapter Written By Jennifer Webb

Note: This section is the reflection of someone who learned the trauma prayer in the context of the Healing Rooms we established through our local church, experienced what it did for her and is now using it to great effect in the context of women's prison ministry that she and her husband now operate out of that same church. The power of this piece is that she has woven it into what she knows and how she ministers, and consequently, is very effective with it. It is not important that you pray this prayer process point-by-point. It is important that you pray for others. — Jim

I (Jennifer) use the trauma prayer process, or a reasonable facsimile thereof, in the facilities where my husband and I are currently ministering. One is a medium security state prison for women and the other is a state run substance abuse treatment center, also for women.

In this type of ministry, significant trauma, either as an event or on a long-term systematic basis, is a common part of the history of these residents. Drug rehab facilities are very similar in population to the prisons and the residents are affected by trauma in much the same way.

We had one inmate in the prison that had been held hostage and stabbed over a dozen times. Another had gasoline deliberately poured on her and was set ablaze. God miraculously healed her face and her ability to walk, but inside she still carries the scars of the trauma she experienced. These are just two examples of hundreds of women in only one facility. The stories of abuse are similar in the substance abuse treatment center. In these populations, trauma is often a generational issue, coupled with the need for forgiveness and the breaking of soul ties. For many, the patterns of abuse initiated the addictions, and the addictions themselves created another level of unresolved trauma.

The power of forgiveness needs to be taught, for we have learned that we cannot assume that they know the effects of forgiveness, or understand the results of unforgiveness. Without understanding of true forgiveness, many struggle with being able to forgive, which may block the legal rights to remove trauma and all associated attachments and bring other forms of deliverance. Many of them believe that if they forgive, they are in effect saying that what was done to them was okay.

Another closely related issue has to do with the formation of soul ties with the individual who violated them. Often they have been in relationship with those who have abused them. Be aware of these related needs as you minister to individuals in similar situations.

Without understanding of true forgiveness, many struggle with being able to forgive, which may block the legal rights to remove trauma and all associated attachments and bring other forms of deliverance.

As is usual, addiction is a large part of their personal battle. As for the state prisoners, their addictions run the spectrum from individuals to emotions, substances, gambling, high risk excitement, you name it. The substance abuse rehab facility is the last stop for ladies prior to prison. This is a pass/fail environment. Dealing effectively with the results of trauma that each of these women has experienced has been our key to getting to their hearts. They have experienced relief from some of the symptoms of trauma as they have allowed us to pray over them in a corporate environment. That's opened a major door for us individually.

Ministering healing for trauma corporately

We have found that this type of ministry, e.g., ministry to a specific, emotionally-charged issue, is very effective for particular outreaches we do, such as at the prison or drug rehab.

On one recent evening in the prison, we had 87 women in attendance. Before starting and during intercession, one of our groups got a picture of a waterfall. I knew it was for cleansing. Next, we saw a cesspool and knew that as the Lord was cleansing the women much would be going "down the drain" not to return to them. We shared this with the women which created an expectation in them. During worship, the Lord revealed through a word of knowledge that He wanted to heal some specific wounds. These had to do with being shot, stabbed, strangled, or raped.

Being led by Holy Spirit, I had the women close their eyes due to the personal nature of what we would be dealing with. I then had them stand as each type of the four wounds was called out. The number who had been raped was significant. One woman wrote later on her prayer/communication card that she had been raped over 30 times. Of the 87 attending that night, probably 35 stood to receive healing concerning these specific traumatic issues. I believe there were more who could have stood.

The prayer was led by Holy Spirit so it was unscripted but held these basic elements:

Addressing specific wound(s). We spoke healing to the physical body and blessed it with healing. (Often with this I will see the physical wound in the spirit and address tissue repair or whatever Holy Spirit reveals – be sensitive to what you are seeing or hearing.)

Speaking to the soul. The Lord addressed the thoughts, memories and emotions, commanding trauma to leave. Often, the adrenaline released at that original occurrence can be triggered again by memories of the events, so the "adrenaline rush" needs to be addressed, called back into balance, and sometimes forbidden from reoccurring, etc.

Forgiveness. After this part of the prayer at the prison, the Lord revealed that forgiveness needed to happen before some would be released. A brief explanation of the power of forgiveness was given. Specifically, the points being: by choosing to forgive, the recipient would be released from torment; and by stepping out of the judgment, God could address these issues with the person(s) who had committed these violations. I invited them to pray a "repeat after me" type forgiveness prayer that they could personalize as they went through it.

I walked them through another repeat-after-me prayer covering the aspect of forgiveness directed toward God, and to release God from judgments held against Him. In the process, the Lord explained that He was not the author of these events or actions. He said the real enemy was the one who comes to "steal, kill, and destroy". He spoke to them briefly about the "accuser of the brethren" who accuses Him to them as well as them to others, etc.

Removing trauma. Next came more commanding of trauma and all attachments and assignments to leave every part of them, to go to the feet of Jesus and go only where He commanded, not returning to the person.

Blessing the spirit. This is an important part of the healing process. I bless their spirits to come alive, to rise up and hear Holy Spirit, or whatever the Lord desires them to have deposited in the spirit part of them. God then reminded them of who they are and the plans He has for them.

Sealing of ministry. Sealing in the work is an important final step. A sealing prayer was prayed declaring the doors that God had shut would remain shut, pleading Jesus' blood over each recipient – spirit, soul, and body.

Ministering healing for trauma to an individual in an altar-type setting

Ministry sometimes occurs differently when someone has come for prayer at an altar or for an altar call. One often has less time to minister and one does not know if you will have another chance to minister to this person. So hearing the voice of God in these settings is really important.

An example of the importance of hearing the Lord prophetically when ministering this way happened about a week ago during altar ministry at our church. A 21 year-old young man from out of town came to me for prayer. He admitted he'd not been inside a church for years. He said he'd come to this area to reconcile with his father. He then shared that he'd been in dangerous situations and had been shot three times. He had come to the realization that he could not go on without help.

As I listened to both him and Holy Spirit, I first ministered salvation to him which is the biggest miracle and an important factor to know so that you are not wrestling against things in the spirit unnecessarily.

I realized God wanted to minister to the trauma received by the gunshot wounds he'd mentioned. As I prayed concerning that specific trauma, the Lord revealed that he had also been stabbed. When I spoke this out, the young man shook his head in amazement since he had not said anything about being stabbed.

Again, I ministered the release of trauma in a similar pattern outlined previously, but as much as that, the healing he received from the prophetic ministry of salvation and hearing the Father's heart for him, according to his step-mother who had brought him, was totally life changing.

The other day a neighbor stopped by with a sore arm and wrist after a motorcycle accident the night before. I prayed over him and simply asked Jesus, "Please remove all effects of trauma from him." (Nothing detailed, simply that). He started crying, leaned forward and whispered in my ear that he wanted Jesus in his heart." We led him to receive Jesus and then in a prayer to forgive everyone, one-by-one who had hurt him.

Also, two months ago prayed over another young man on medication for "brain problems" as he put it - struggling with school. Again, asked Jesus to remove the effects of trauma - again, just that simple prayer. Two weeks later he said his studies had improved and he realized his parents really did love him (Wow! He hadn't mentioned that part to me!). Then to top it off I was talking with his principal at school a few days later and he made a comment to me..."I don't know what has happened with that young man, but it's like he is a different kid!"

Finally, I prayed the same simple prayer over another young man and when we were through he said he saw hooks coming out of his head, hands and feet!

Ministering to Returning War Veterans

What you can do for them is cut off the horrific torment that always haunts the days and nights of trauma survivors.

As stated earlier, this ministry manual is a collection of tools that was originally intended to be directed to another group of trauma victims: survivors of sex trafficking. But, there is perhaps no greater need with which we are currently faced than that of the returning service man/woman injured as a result of combat operations in Iraq or Afghanistan. If for no other reason, this is true because of the sheer numbers of American service men and women who have served one or more tours of duty there.

As stated in the following statistics, the number of sufferers of symptoms related to Post Traumatic Stress Disorder (PTSD) and Traumatic Brain Injury (TBI), due to being in close proximity to the explosion of a roadside bomb and other combat action, among active duty service men and women is high, but the statistics for those who were called up from National Guard posts are nothing short of alarming. These symptoms include a very high incidence of depression, mental illness, substance abuse and suicide and are very typical for combat soldiers. One of the things that makes these statistics still more alarming is the fact that the reporting of these mental health issues require the individual themselves to seek help, and they must do it at a Veterans Hospital or Community Life facility established for such purposes. They are not necessarily convenient to a 20-something vet. Consequently, the military believes that as high as these statistics are, they are probably significantly under-reported.

Because these individuals come from towns all over America, large and small, there are likely a number of them living and working among you who are struggling with the after effects of having waged a killing war on foreign soil. With each succeeding year the number of them increases. The probability of one of these folks, who are struggling to make it, living next door to you, is growing rapidly.

The Trauma Prayer Process was created for just such situations. It was written in step form to make it easy for you to follow the direction of Holy Spirit as you move from topic to topic. The other tools provided will help you help them resolve the open doors to fear and helplessness, and uncover and dispose of lies planted by the enemy which have blown apart their internal peace and safety.

This does not mean that they have no need for the mental health professionals that are available to them through the Veterans Administration because you're on the job. There are times and situations where the complexity of issues is such that the services of a professional are warranted, if only to provide them appropriate medication that will allow them to function until the issues are resolved.

What you can do for them is cut off the horrific torment that always haunts the days and nights of trauma survivors. By your simple intervention, you have the power to save a life, and in doing so, you will shorten their recuperative process for the victim and their families.

The subsequent statistics will give a broad understanding of what the problem entails and how pervasive it is.

Statistics for Returning War Veterans[32]
- 1.7 million service members and veterans to deploy in support of the Operation Iraqi

Freedom/Operation Enduring Freedom (OIF/OEF).

- A recent RAND Corporation study titled "Invisible Wounds: Mental Health and Cognitive Care Needs of America's Returning Veterans" found that an estimated 1 out of 5 of all service members, or 18.5%, suffer from PTSD or some form of major depression.

- The study also found that "53 percent of returning troops who met criteria for PTSD or major depression sought help from a provider for these conditions in the past year."

- As of December 2008, more than 4,000 troops have been killed and over 30,000 have returned from a combat zone with visible wounds and a range of permanent disabilities.

- In addition, an estimated 25-40 percent have less visible wounds—psychological and neurological injuries associated with post traumatic stress disorder (PTSD) or traumatic brain injury (TBI), which have been dubbed "signature injuries" of the Iraq War.

- SAMHSA and the National Institute for Drug Abuse have repeatedly concluded that PTSD and depression are both risk factors for substance abuse, and in some cases, suicide. The VA recently testified before Congress that the suicide rate among OIF/OEF veterans under

VA care from 2002 to 2005 was 17.0 per 100,000 compared to 24.0 per 100,000 for such veterans who were not enrolled with the VA.

- Returning veterans with mental health and substance abuse problems may run into problems in other areas of their lives such as homelessness and unemployment, or worse, crime or suicide. One-third of the nation's homeless individuals are veterans.
- Left untreated, individuals with substance abuse and/or mental health disorders pose significant financial risks to communities that are already in the midst of budget reductions.
- Currently, veterans have a higher rate of suicide ranging from 17.5 to 22.0 per 100,000 as compared to the general population of 11.0 per 100,000 nationally.
- A study in the 2007 Journal of Epidemiology and Community Health vii reported that male veterans are twice as likely to die by suicide as non-military men.
- There is nearly a 20% increase in confirmed active-duty suicides since 2006, according to an internal US Army report.
- In 2006, the suicide rate in the US Army reached its highest level in 26 years.

- Studies have concluded that homeless veterans are at a higher risk than the general population for mental illness, substance abuse, and suicide.
- Of the 1.7 million troops that have served in Iraq and Afghanistan since the beginning of the conflicts, 799,800 have been discharged and eligible for VA care and 299,600 have gone to the VA for care. Of those 299,600, suffering from PTSD is an approximate 59,800 while the number suffering from all mental disorders is estimated at 120,000.
- The second most common health concern, second only to musculoskeletal ailments (joint and back disorders), is mental disorders.
- From 15-20% of all soldiers fighting in Iraq and Afghanistan show signs of depression or post traumatic stress disorder, based on a study of almost 2,300 soldiers finished last fall. That rate jumps to about 30% for soldiers who have been on three or four combat deployments.
- More than one quarter of US soldiers on their third or fourth tours in Iraq suffer mental health problems partly because troops are not getting enough time at home between deployments, the US Army said.
- Recent data from the Defense Medical Surveillance System reflecting self-assessments since June 2005 of service members who had

served in Iraq, shows that 50% of US Army National Guardsmen and some 45% of US Army and Marine reservists have reported mental health concerns.

- Of those using VA health care, 30% suffer from depressive symptoms, 2-3 times the rate of the general population.

- According to the National Survey on Drug Use and Health Report, one quarter of veterans age 25 and under suffered from substance abuse disorders in the preceding year. Substance abuse disorders remain one of the three top diagnoses in the VA system (Dr. Richard T. Suchinsky, DVA, Chief for Addictive Disorders).

High Rate of PTSD in Returning Iraq War Veterans[33]

Evan Kanter, MD, PhD, staff psychiatrist in the PTSD Outpatient Clinic of the VA Puget Sound Health Care System, said that estimates are for a minimum of 300,000 psychiatric casualties from service in Iraq up to this point, with an estimated lifetime cost of treatment of $660 billion. That is more than the actual cost of the war to date ($500 billion).

"A study of the first 100,000 [Iraq and Afghanistan] veterans seen at VA facilities showed that 25% of them received mental health diagnoses. Of these,

56% had two or more mental health diagnoses. The most common were PTSD, substance abuse, and depression," Dr. Kanter said. "The younger the veterans are, the more likely they are to have mental health conditions."

Evaluation immediately on return from deployment suggested that 5% of active duty and 6% of reserve personnel had a significant mental health problem. When reassessed three to six months later, 27% of active duty and 42% of reserve personnel received that evaluation.

Dr. Kanter said there are two reasons for that difference: "At the time of return, people want to get home and get to their families. They perceive that if they answer yes to the question, it is going to take time [and delay their return home]. So, there is tremendous underreporting. The other is that PTSD and other mental health conditions have an insidious and delayed onset."

The official 17 symptoms of PTSD can be placed into three broad groups:

- Re-experiencing: intrusive memories, nightmares, flashbacks, triggered distress;
- Avoidance: isolation, withdrawal, emotional numbing, detachment, memory gaps; and

- Hyper-arousal: insomnia, irritability, anger outbursts, poor concentration, hyper-vigilance, exaggerated startle.

Beyond the official diagnosis are associated features that result in poor occupational and social function. They include depression, suicidal ideation, alcohol and drug abuse, guilt, shame, inability to trust, over-controlling, few or no close relationships, extreme isolation, unemployment, divorce, domestic violence, and child abuse.

Within the general population, going back to World War I, combat veterans historically are twice as likely to die of suicide as the non-veteran. Within the current Army, the rate of suicide is the highest it has been in the 26 years that records have been kept.

"The younger the veterans are, the more likely they are to have mental health conditions." – Dr. Kanter

"One of the risk factors for PTSD is the unprecedented multiple deployments [to a combat zone]," Dr. Kanter observed. The intensity and duration of the trauma predicts PTSD. "There is a dose response. People who have been multiply deployed are much sicker, and it is going to be more costly to take care of them." More than a half million persons have been deployed two or more times.

The effect on families also is great. "You see more marital problems, more behavioral problems in children, more family violence, and the potential for the generational transmission of violence. In the Vietnam cohort, those with PTSD were 3 to 6 times more likely to get divorced," he commented.

Dr. Kanter is guardedly hopeful that a greater understanding of PTSD and earlier intervention will result in better outcomes than those seen from the Vietnam era, but significant barriers to accessing care remain.

Perhaps the most difficult obstacle to overcome is the attitude of the typical 20-something solider returning to civilian life. "It is hard to get a 22-year-old to come in to see the doctor for any reason," Dr. Kanter noted. "The stigma of PTSD and mental illness in general runs very high. There also is a lot of distrust, avoidance, and denial that are inherent in the disorder. People are worried about their military careers and that if they get a mental health diagnosis, they will be drummed out."

Ministering Freedom

1. Interview

This step is going to be an especially important part of this process because the sources of trauma in the life of the veteran may well have begun long before their entry into the military. It would be helpful to know if they are in any way connected to those experiences as a function of military life. If physical injuries accompanied any of the traumatic events, make certain to note the country in which they occurred because it will come in handy as you enter Step 2. Be sure to ask questions about rehabilitative surgeries and procedures in the process. Demonic entities love to be able to use the "twilight" time between full unconsciousness due to anesthesia and full consciousness as an opportunity to open the door for fear.

2. Disconnect from the 2nd Heaven

In addition to disconnecting the veteran from entities that gained access to them via the trauma, you will need to separate them from access by another group that is related to the country in which they served.

We have been most fortunate here in the United States that, save the Revolutionary War, which served to establish our union, and the Civil War, which attempted to tear it apart, all of the wars and conflicts that U.S. military personnel have participated in have been conducted on foreign soil. American servicemen/women are stationed everywhere the U.S. has an embassy, and everywhere that we have a base (Philippines, Japan, Belgium, Germany, Turkey, Greece, Saudi Arabia, Spain, Portugal, England, Italy, Malaysia, Bahrain, Afghanistan, Iraq, Bulgaria, Kuwait, Kosovo, Netherlands, Puerto Rico, Qatar, South Korea, United Kingdom), not to mention anywhere the C.I.A. has some covert operation.

The negative side of that is when a soldier is on foreign soil, he/she comes under the influence of the powers and principalities over those nations. Iraq and Afghanistan boast some of the most ancient spirits since they are effectively the cradle of civilization on this planet.

Below are some of the prominent influences to deal with[34]:

Romantic peoples (Greece, Italy, France, Spain) generally deal with the spirit of the Midianites, i.e., on a journey of contention, strife and quarreling. They also face the influence of the Amorite spirit which represents bitterness, rebellion, babbling, lust and those who operate through publicity and positions of honor for the purpose of recognition.

Germanic peoples (Germany, Belgium, Poland, Austria, and Czechoslovakia) deal with the spirit of Moab and/or Sidon, i.e., pride, pride in their own glory. Germanic peoples also have to deal with another curse because of the pride issue. It is a spirit of defeatism. The Word says, *"Pride goes before destruction, and a haughty spirit before stumbling."*[35] That's happened over and over again, particularly in Germany and the Czech Republic. One of the possible ways to recognize the defeatist spirit in operation is that the defeatist spirit causes all manner of addictions.

Egyptians, by name, are defined as, "he that troubles or oppresses; one that produces anguish (worry, anxiety, anger and despair)."

Jordan / Saudi Arabia: Moabites – arrogance, pride, insolence[36]; defeatism. Moab was the product of an incestuous union of Lot and his oldest daughter.[37]

Turkey / Romania / Bulgaria / Armenia / Azerbaijan / Georgia: Hittites – "one who is broken; who fears (fear and depression)." Jebusites – "trodden under foot (defeatism, helpless, hopeless)."

Iraq / Iran / Afghanistan / Pakistan / India – Persian prince.[38]

What is listed above are essentially the spirits which were behind the enemies of Israel. With the changes in political and agricultural climates, people often moved to find more suitable circumstances taking their gods with them. Hence, those gods whose influence at one time was relegated to a fairly small people group now has multiplied influence because of exposure to additional people groups.

Here are a few that are hard to classify because so many people groups exhibit some of these characteristics:

- **Canaanites** – merchant; trader; or he that humbles and subdues (poverty)
- **Girgashites** – he who arrives from pilgrimage (exhaustion)
- **Hivites** – wicked; wickedness (rebellion, perversion, defilement)
- **Kenites** – possession; purchase; lamentation
- **Ammonites** – Ammon was the product of an incestuous union of Lot and his youngest daughter.[39]

You might even ask the Lord, "Are there any curses that affect them that come down through Abraham's lineage?"

- **Ham** – Egypt, North Africa, Berbers, Tunisia, Sudan
- **Japheth** – Germany, Europe, Picts, Celts, Ostrogoths, Visigoths, Goths, Vandals, Scandinavians, Teutons, Franks, Dutch,

Russians, Kurds, Indians, Iranians, Greeks, Romans, Spaniards, Cossacks
- **Shem** – Persia, Assyria, Iraq, Arabia, Palestinians, Asia Minor, Northern Africa, Syrians, Asia, Middle East

Unfortunately, I don't have experience with many folks from Asia, Africa, South or Central America, so I can't offer any suggestions as to what you may be dealing with in the way of ancestral ruling spirits. If you have an experience in this arena, I would greatly appreciate any correspondence so that we can pass along this information to those who need it.

A Vietnamese Curse

Here's one bit of information for ministry to those who fought in the Vietnam Conflict. It is a Vietnamese-Buddhist curse against Americans. In Vietnam, a country dominated by Buddhism, Hinduism, and Spiritism, pagan spiritual powers and sorcerers ruled villages, directed battles, and were called upon to destroy opponents. According to an ex-Buddhist priest, an entire sect of Vietnamese-Buddhist monks spent years diligently praying and invoking the following curses upon all Americans that came into their country: *that American soldiers would become wandering men for the rest of their lives; that they would never find peace; and that they would be angry people for the rest of their lives.*

Breaking the Vietnamese Buddhist Curse

"In the name of the Lord Jesus Christ, I break the curse made against me by the Buddhist(s) that said I would wander the rest of my life, that I would never find peace and that I would be angry for the rest of my life. I call upon the name of the Lord my God to restore the blessings of peace, safety and rest in my life."

The Rest

The remainder of the steps are pretty much the same as noted in the first chapters (see "Freedom from Trauma"), except you will need to pay specific attention to commanding the body to release the memory of all sensory elements connected with traumatic injury such as smells, temperature, humidity, tastes, sensations, premonitions, vibrations, etc., anything Holy Spirit suggests that was connected or compiled in memories of those events.

I got a call yesterday from a lady who had visited the church with her husband the day you spoke about healing the soul. She came up front for ministry afterwards and wanted the trauma prayer prayed over her for the effects of mono that she has been experiencing for a long time. We prayed the best we could. Her call was to let us know that it had powerfully impacted her and she was feeling great – which goes to show you that you don't have to know the entire Trauma Prayer by heart. This is the first time we have had personal feedback in ministering like that and I thought it would encourage you to know how God used you that Sunday.

Ungodly Ties of the Soul

"And he said, 'For this cause shall a man leave father and mother, and shall cleave to his wife: and they two shall be one flesh.'" – Matthew 19:5 (KJV)

Godly ties of the soul have their foundation in the first sexual union of man and woman. That relationship was ordained by God to be a perpetually monogamous relationship, which was not initiated by a local official, nor by a ceremony, but by the act of sexual union. Sexual union was originally designed to be the greatest act of intimacy one human can enter into with another, symbolizing the gift of self to another without boundaries (symbolized by nakedness). Prior to the union of these two (Adam & Eve, that is), there were no experimental relationships on their part, and no unions of comfort, convenience or sport. This wasn't just because they were the only two on the planet. It was because God was painting a picture of the perfect for all eternity.

Genesis 2:21-24 (NKJV):

> *"And the LORD God caused a deep sleep to fall upon Adam, and he slept; and he took one of his ribs, and closed up the flesh instead thereof; And the rib, which the LORD God had taken from man, made he a woman, and brought her unto the man. And Adam said, 'This is now bone of my bones, and flesh of my flesh: she shall be called Woman, because she was taken out of Man. Therefore shall a man leave his father and his mother, and shall cleave unto his wife: and they shall be one flesh.'"*

Matthew 19:5-6 (KJV; emphasis added):

> *"And he said, 'For this cause shall a man leave father and mother, and shall cleave to his wife: and they two shall be one flesh. Wherefore <u>they are no more two, but one flesh</u>. What therefore God hath joined together, let not man put asunder.'"*

The concept of **"one"** flesh is important because the act of sexual union bonds two together in the arena of the soul (the mind, will and emotions) for life. This is the soul tie. Many individuals have entered into a soul tie as the result of a sexual union with one or more partners prior to marriage, between marriages, or as adultery during marriage. Those who are in the sex trade find themselves creating them on a daily basis. Just because it is forced, or considered as work, doesn't alter the consequence.

In 2 Corinthians 6: 14-16 (KJV), Paul wrote:

> *"Be not unequally yoked together with unbelievers: for what fellowship hath righteousness with unrighteousness? And what communion hath light with darkness? And what concord hath Christ with Belial? Or what part hath he that believeth with an infidel? And what agreement hath the temple of God with idols? For you are the temple of the living God; as God hath said, I will dwell in them, and walk in them; and I will be their God, and they shall be my people."*

The concept here, although directed to believers, is also applicable for non-believers as well. Why should you continue to maintain a tie to those who paid to abuse you and those who forced you into it? Separate from them as far as possible. It is also a call to those who would like God to help them to resolve the internal conflict caused by their self-destructive activities.

1 Corinthians 6:15 (RSV; emphasis added): *"Do you not know that your bodies are members of Christ?*

Shall I therefore take the members of Christ and **make them members of** *a prostitute? Never! Do you not know that he who joins himself to a prostitute becomes* **one body with her?** *For as it is written, '***The two shall become one flesh***.'"*

Whether we were believers or not at the time the soul tie was made, we *were* "yoked" or joined or made one (spirit, body and soul) with unbelievers. The term 'prostitute' in this verse is unfortunate for those who are trying to escape the trade, but in the Biblical sense, it carries with it the idea of intentionally connecting yourself with someone who is defiled. Hence, the viewpoint that this is a very poor decision indeed.

The effect of multiple sexual unions creates a difficulty in fully being able to freely give ourselves to God, or to anyone else, because so many others have a piece of us. And since we have become one with them, we have also become one with whatever defilement they have been a part of. In extreme cases, people with multiple soul ties have great difficulty making decisions because they are pulled in so many directions by those they are connected to.

For someone who has multiple sexual unions in a single night, repeated over many nights, the results are significant. When multiplied by the other issues created by pimps and violent clients, it is no wonder that the life expectancy of those involved in the sex trade is no more than 6 years.

Manipulative Ties

Another very prominent form of the soul tie is that created with manipulative and controlling authority figures with whom there was a very close personal relationship. These can be as devastating as sexual unions because through covert forms of witchcraft, the emotional and soulish bonds became just as close. The fact that there is also a common spiritual relationship often is used to camouflage and confuse the other issues.

Heart Ties

Another form is found in the bond formed when an individual falls in love with another, particularly in teen years. Although there may never have been any sexual union, or perhaps no control exerted, the heart was completely given and was never fully taken back. So the tie remains unbroken. I often see this when someone comes to me wondering why their spouse of 20 years is jealous when they are exchanging messages on Facebook[40] with their high school sweetheart of 25 years ago. There is apparently still more there than simple curiosity.

If there are any affections of the heart which compete with our affections for the Lord, they need to be identified and properly dealt with.

I cannot prove this Biblically, but there is apparently a very strong bond formed with your "first love" which is connected to the initial awakening of the most powerful force within any human being: the desire to be loved in return by the object of your affection. It is certainly obvious to those who experienced it that it was without doubt the most powerful, most moving, most engrossing and all-encompassing feeling ever experienced to date, evoking over-the-top emotional reactions to everything. The world could not be a more wonderful place in which to live if we were just able to hang on to all those feelings that flooded us with our "first love." Needless to say, that needs to be cut.

Another element of heart ties is the flip side of what was just discussed – that which involves other visceral type emotions which tend to maintain connections with another individual that is not welcomed. These are especially linked to the results of unforgiveness, animosity, hatred, harboring of bitterness and murder in the heart, etc. Quite frequently, we find that spouses who have endured betrayal and abandonment willingly deal with the sexual side of the soul tie, but have a more difficult time cutting their attachment to the offending spouse made possible through the offense they have maintained.

If there are any affections of the heart which compete with our affections for the Lord, they need to be identified and properly dealt with. We are not talking about love for our spouses and children, unless they are unhealthy and prevent us from connecting properly with Holy Spirit.

Ties of Submission

There are also soul ties formed when one willfully submits his/her personhood to that of another for the purpose of instruction, mentoring, apprenticeship, etc., Christian or otherwise. In the case of believers, the individual needs to cut only the ungodly tie that exists between the two. This has been experienced with several young people who have been mentored by godly men. The relationship was holy, but on occasion, what was passed along was simply the traditions of men that bound the young believer to dispensational principles that would not allow them to enter into what God had for them now. In these cases, break the ungodly and leave the godly intact.

Blood Oaths

Typically, we find these ties having been made sometimes quite innocently during childhood as a fanciful means of bonding with other dear friends around a specific purpose or "brotherhood". Others were made as a part of some cultic ceremony. Still others have been made in order to be part of some group or institution. God views oaths ratified in blood very seriously, having done the same for you and I in the blood of His own son. These must be broken and any promises or vows spoken during the ceremony individually broken and recanted. Release must be pronounced for all parties to the oath.

Parental Ties

Parental ties are often hard to break when we become adults. We sometimes find that after living apart from mom and dad 20 or more years, we still fall back into the same old patterns when we come home for a visit. Part of this is natural, for you will always be the son or daughter, and they, mom and dad, until you die. The love and concern parents have for children cannot be stamped out. However, at some point, the parent-child relationship should naturally mature from strictly being a parent to one of peer, friend or confidant.

Many grew into adulthood, but the maturing of the parent-child relationship never managed to make the transition. The parent never chose to move from 'source' to 'resource'. Almost all of us can relate to the experience of coming home for a visit for a week or more and everyone resuming the roles they each had when the child lived at home full-time. Some adults still attempt to hang onto being the controlling, manipulative parents they always were, particularly if there was parental inversion involved.

When you get married, the scripture tells us that we leave our father and mother and *become* (the inference from the Greek word) glued to your spouse.[41] Any ungodly glue that still connects you with your parents needs to be scrubbed off.

Note: Honoring your father and mother is a command of scripture and it is vital for our well-being that we observe it. You also have to understand that honoring your parents looks differently at the various seasons of life. Obedience to your parents at age 18 necessarily changes by the time you are 28, 38 and 48. Don't get relationally stuck in a season for the rest of your life.

Breaking Ungodly Soul Ties
Deliverance is a matter of the confession of each union (by name) as sin, repenting for the sin, renouncing the union, breaking the union (agreement) and its effect in your life in the name

of Jesus, and asking forgiveness for the union in behalf of the partner. Call any pieces of your soul back to you, so that you can be whole again and release the other's soul to them so they can be whole as well. Then bless them and all their relationships. Bless them with health and a strong hunger for righteousness.

It may look something like this (where there are blanks, insert the name of the person being prayed over):

"Father, in the name of Jesus, I recant and renounce, break, shatter and destroy all ungodly soul ties between me and _____. I ask your forgiveness for entering into such a union and ask for the forgiveness of the other party for the part I played in establishing this ungodly tie. Father, I ask that you separate me from any second heaven entity that I agreed with by entering into this union; and I ask that you break every curse established against me and break the assignment of every familiar spirit assigned to me and my family line as a result of entering into this union. I further ask, Father, that you disconnect me from any idol or demonic entity that my partner worshipped at the time and remove from me any defilement resulting from my connection with them. I call back to myself anything of me (soul or spirit) that

_____ still retains; and I send back to _____ anything of them that I still hold on to. I ask, Father, that you make each of us whole persons again, able to fully worship and commune with you in spirit and in truth."

Many times you will encounter someone who is struggling with flashbacks, or the like, and have gone through the process of repenting for those unholy unions. Repentance is only part of the process. Breaking each soul tie and praying healing for their fractured and damaged heart will complete the process for them.

If there are other issues such as rape, perversion, recurring images, etc., handle it if there is time, or arrange a separate time for prayer for deliverance and inner healing. The Presenting Jesus tool, which is part of the Sozo ministry technique, is most effective in dealing with such issues.

Your new book is fabulous - I cannot put it down. Reading it I had an amazing vision/visitation from the Lord that I would love to share with you. A somehow super accelerated healing happening when I started praying about being rejected in the womb by my mother. I shared the experience at our church Sunday a.m. and caused a run on your book.

I think I will be using your book as a personal prayer tool for a very long time and think the results will be the best as of yet. Personally, I think the two most important events of the last year for the Body of Christ are the Bay of the Holy Spirit Revival in Mobile, AL and the publishing of your book – "The Effects of Trauma and How to Deal With It."

Love: The Greater Force

Chapter written by Becca Wineka

There is no greater force in the universe than love. Love created. Love breathed life. Love begat love. Love believes, hopes, and endures. Love never fails. There is something about love that is fierce and there is a force behind it – God Almighty. He is Love. True love is what the world is crying out for and the human soul longing for. Love is the conduit to living and the glory of God is man fully alive.

I (Becca) had a dream in 2008 at a point when God was bringing revelation to my heart about His love. In the dream, two people were getting married. One person was really small in size and the other was very large, having a golden appearance.

Looking at the extreme size differences, I wondered, "How is this going to work? How are they going to consummate their marriage?" Then, a third figure appeared and came in between the two people. When this happened, the large, golden person became smaller, converting to the same size as the other person so that they could be together and be a fit. The third figure stayed over top of them, serving as a sort of mantle or covering, so they could remain together and the relationship was then consummated.

This dream speaks on so many levels of the surrounding, covering nature of love. It reveals the heart of God is to be with us, to be intimate. Without the covering in the dream, the two figures were unable to fit together and experience oneness. Hebrews 1:3 says, *"The Son is the radiance of God's glory and the exact representation of his being, sustaining all things by his powerful word."* Jesus and the Father are One and the Holy Spirit of God within a reborn human brings man into the same oneness with God that Jesus has. This is the kind of intimacy and union we were created for in the heart of God. We were created by God who is love and for He who is love.

Love is the tangible substance that brings change to people's lives. The work of transformation from the inside out begins in receiving God's love for us.

In John 3, Jesus talks with Nicodemus about being born again of water and of the Spirit. He told Nicodemus that the Holy Spirit is like the wind in which one can see the effects of the wind, yet not know where it came from or where it is going. Love has some similar characteristics. It, too, shares invisible, yet tangibly affecting qualities. Love has rebirthing qualities to it because it is powerful and it is alive; it has substance. Love is God and God is love.

Whenever a life came into contact with Jesus, *change ensued.* The needs of people were met; their hearts were forgiven, healed, set free from the demonic, resurrected from the dead, and all together transformed through encountering the raw force of Jesus' love for them. The people were like sheep without a shepherd and His heart was moved towards them with compassion, even those who would turn away.[42]

So what does this mean for us as the Body of Christ? The Bible says the world knows that we are His disciples by how we love one another. Love and the finished work of the cross are the keys to all healing. We are called to be conduits of His love and this happens as we encounter His inexhaustibly deep love for us personally and healing ensues. We are to love one another with

His love for us and we all know we can't muster up that kind of love because it's supernatural!

The foundations of the world and the Word of God are laid upon Love.[43] Before the foundations of the world, love triumphed, for the Lamb of God was slain before any of it came to be.[44] It is this kind of love that set time and space in motion at creation. It is the finished work of the cross of Jesus Christ of Nazareth who demonstrated the Father's love for us in that while we were still sinners, Christ died for us.[45] Love always wins and leads a triumphal procession![46]

Love has rebirthing qualities to it because it is powerful and it is alive; it has substance

One time, in a vision, I heard the Lord say, *"If you want to understand the beginning, go to the end."* I came to see that if I was to understand Genesis 1-2 and this "face-to-face" relationship that God longs to have with each of us, I had to go to the book of Revelation. I came to realize that God provided the lamb before time began and that the Lamb was Jesus who *"with your blood you purchased man for God."*[47] God Himself would lay aside His glory and lay down His life to which there is no greater love.[48] He rescued us from the peril of the most detrimental day in history in which we could no longer commune with God face-to-face – the fall.

That is what the foundation of this book has been about – LOVE and the finished work of the Cross of Jesus Christ.[49]

In order for the tools in it to be effective, ask God to cultivate a heart of love in you so that through it you can stand in the authority of Christ's finished work by the power of His Spirit, calling the "Lazarus" in front of you out of the grave and commanding that the grave clothes be removed. It is about coming into agreement with Isaiah 61 and Jesus' heart for those He loves – the poor, brokenhearted, captives, prisoners, the mourning and grieving, and the despairing. Ministering healing is about standing in agreement with the *"it is finished"* work of the cross on behalf of those whom Jesus loves, the lost and broken.

We trust the power and work of the Holy Spirit in you and in us to minister out of His heart, out of His love, to whomever He puts in front of you!

This is our prayer:

"Father God, you have given us the greatest gift and fullest expression of Your love in Your Son, Jesus. Holy Spirit, fill us afresh as we fix our

eyes on Jesus, the Author and Perfector of our faith; the Lover of our spirits, souls, and bodies. Burst forth in our hearts and bring the height, length, width and depth of Jesus' love for us that we may love others as You have loved us. Deepen those roots in us, Holy Spirit, that we may be established in the love that Papa God has for us. Father, we pray that those You put before us to love and minister to would know Your heartbeat of love, be set free from captivity, have grave clothes removed, be healed by Your Word, and become oaks of righteousness for Your Glory and Name's sake. Transform us by Your relentless and pursuing love for which we are thankful! Release the roar of Your love over us, Jesus, for Your Name's Sake! Amen."

Appendix A: The Effects of Trauma and How to Deal With It - Abbreviated Version

1. *Interview*

Through specific questions, usually an interview, determine the traumatic events for the client from childhood into adulthood (physical, emotional, spiritual, sexual). Inquire about such things as divorce, deaths, loss of a key loved one, childhood accidents and injuries, rape, abuse, surgeries, frequent moves, moves at key times, major rejections, abandonment, car accidents, major illnesses, broken bones, losses, surgeries and invasive medical procedures, attempted suicide, near death experiences, etc. – anything that potentially had a major negative (traumatic) effect on them. Make a list if you need to.

2. Disconnect From the 2nd Heaven

This is important. Ask the Lord to disconnect them from any and all 2nd heaven entities – principalities, powers, dominions, thrones, rulers, etc. – that have gained access to them through the traumatic events they have suffered for the purpose of future torment.

3. Body Release

Next, get their permission to take authority over their being/body for a few minutes to cut some things off. Begin by commanding all of the residual effects of trauma, whether it be physical, emotional or spiritual, to be released.

Be certain to include the effects of all abuse, defiling touch, incisions, invasive medical procedures, rape, violent car accidents, major injuries, near-death experiences, rejections, abandonment, beatings/bruises, harsh words or curses spoken by parents or other significant authorities, etc. In the event of a particularly defiling activity such as rape or initial homosexual encounters, command out of their body the memory of all smells, feelings, tastes, sounds, vibrations and defiling touch connected with those events.

4. Body Release: Trauma

Take authority over their physical body and command out of it all of the long and short-term effects of trauma, injuries, stress, tension, worry, anxiety, fear, wounding, etc.

5. *Shut Down Enemy Pathways*

Take authority over all pathways, portals, and means of access, marks or markers, or any means of connectivity placed upon them physically or spiritually to track them or gain access to them for purposes of torment, and shut them down in the authority given to you in the name of Jesus. Ask the Lord to shut down all pathways, portals, and means of 2nd heaven access to them for communication or influence.

Cancel all assignments of familiar spirits made against them as a result of traumatic incidents, or as a result of generational trauma.

6. *Release the Prisoner*

Ask the Lord that if there is any portion of their being that has been delayed, trapped, assigned, captured or imprisoned in another time, another space, dimension or place, as a result of trauma, would He please cause it to be released and rejoined with their core being at this current time, space, dimension and maturity level. I also ask the Lord to re-unify those portions with the core person. I ask the Lord to cleanse those parts of any defilement as a result of where it has been, and to cancel the assignment of any familiar spirit connected to it.

If prompted by the Holy Spirit, walk them through a reunification of these fractured parts by walking them through each dimension or through each year of their lives.

7. Important Declaration

One thing I have discovered while in the midst of praying through the trauma prayer process with women who were traumatized initially as children, and re-traumatized as adults by another means (e.g., auto accident, rape, household robbery) is to direct the following powerful, yet simple "declaration" to their soul and spirit:

"You no longer have to remain on guard, in a heightened state of alertness, or remain in a state of high sensitivity to people or your surroundings. You may now rest and are supposed to enter into a natural state of rest and relaxation. The difficult event(s) is over now. You are no longer in danger. There is no longer a need to remain hyper-sensitive for the sake of personal protection or survival. Those days are over. The danger has passed. You can finally rest. Take a deep breath and exhale slowly."

8. Pray for the Brain

Ask the Lord to reestablish the connection between the hemispheres of the brain. Often, heavily traumatized clients live predominately out of the left hemisphere of their brain and need the right side to be stimulated. Pray that the Lord will reestablish and synchronize both explicit memory and implicit memory and reactivate any connections required to retrieve memories needed for complete healing. Pray that He would bring back into balance all chemical, electrical and magnetic communication paths within the brain and restore them to optimal levels for stability.

9. Destroy Secular Structures

In the name of Jesus, tear down all existing structure of understanding and thought established according to the world's system. These are the mental ideologies, understandings and structures of thoughts taught to us by our ancestors and our immediate family about why things are the way they are (called their truth) and why we should be afraid of them or treat them in a certain fashion. In time, they become your truth, even if it has no resemblance to the real truth and reality of life at all. These are often identified as the family prides and prejudices inherent in a family's line, including such things as misogyny, misandry, denial, poverty, rebellion, isolation, etc.

In the name of Jesus, ask God to establish His Kingdom concepts, structures, principles and understandings over the individual and his/her family line.

10. Restore Sleep Patterns

Ask the Lord to reestablish for them the appropriate sleep patterns the Lord designed for them and to establish for them a sweet, undisturbed, rejuvenating, regenerative rest. Proverbs 3:24 (NASB) – *"When you lie down, you will not be afraid; when you lie down, your sleep will be sweet."*

Ask the Lord to begin or reestablish Godly dreams, visions and angelic visitations in the night seasons, both to enlighten, instruct and direct them.

11. Dismantle the Pushbuttons

Ask the Lord to begin to dismantle all automatic human responses gained as a result of trauma, e.g., abnormal fright responses, triggers, fears and phobias. Pray over their brain for the Lord to rebuild, reestablish, and recreate any electrical or chemical connections broken or improperly re-connected as a result of trauma so that the individual can operate once again within normal limits of high and low stimulus, and can remain in control emotionally when the stimulus exceeds those limits.

12. *Reestablishing Appropriate Time*

As a fellow steward of the earth, you can give the Lord permission to enter into the affairs of men to be redemptive. Simply ask Father to reset the individual's internal time, and the time of all alters and fractures, to the current time – to the current place, domain and space, restoring them to their proper place in time and cleansing the time of any defilement initiated by their sin. Ask the Lord to restore the defiled portion of them to that pre-awakened state, emotionally and physically, removing all defilement of time, defilement of place, domain and space; as well as from them physically, emotionally and spiritually. Ask the Lord to unify all their systems to their current chronological age and maturity level, operating as it would if nothing had been awakened out of time and season.

13. *Connect With God*

Then instruct the client to instruct (tell or direct) his/her human spirit each evening before going to sleep, to turn its face to the Father during the night while the body and soul are out cold, and receive everything he/she needs for the coming day.

14. *Personal Blessing*

I usually close each session with some kind of a blessing. So many people we minister to have never had a real blessing and long to have one. You can write it out and read it to them if you wish, or you and Holy Spirit can wing it. Those are the most fun because you can look them in the eye when you do it. It seems to carry so much more weight with them because eye to eye contact is both intimate and maximizes communication.

Note: I have come to the conclusion that if this prayer process is to have maximum benefit it should be prayed over an individual three (3) times. Things come typically off in layers; so it is with this issue.

End Notes

The Problem

[1] *Strong's Exhaustive Concordance of The Bible*, by James Strong, copyright 2007, by Hendrickson Publishers, Peabody, Massachusetts. Used by permission. All rights reserved.

[2] Baldwin, David. "About Trauma." David Baldwin's Trauma Information Pages. January, 2011

[3] Burk, Arthur. "Inner Healing." Plumline Ministries. January 2011

[4] See Psalm 30:3; 49:15; Isaiah 58:6; 61:1

[5] Restoration in Christ Ministries website: www.rcm-usa.org

[6] "Superstring Theory." Wikipedia, The Free Encyclopedia. Wikimedia Foundation, Inc. 14 January 2011

[7] Papantonopoulos, E. "Brane Cosmology." 2002. National Technical University of Athens, Physics Department, Zografou Campus

[8] See Luke 16:8, Genesis 1:27, 1 John 1:5, and John 1:1-9

[9] See also:

- "Gene melody of Japanese giant salamander is played." - sciencelinks.jp/j-east/article/200510/000020051005A0287630.php

- "A Melody in Your DNA" - www.genealogue.com/2007/07/melody-in-your-dna.html

- "A Cancerous Melody" - www.the-scientist.com/blog/display/55998/

[10] hence the budding science of epi-genetics. See May 17, 2010 Sports Illustrated article titled, "The Sins of the Father"

Freedom from Trauma

[11] Isaiah 14:10-20

[12] John 5:19 – "Jesus gave them this answer: "Very truly I tell you, the Son can do nothing by himself; he can do only what he sees his Father doing, because whatever the Father does the Son also does.""

[13] John 10:10b (NASB). Full text, "The thief comes only to steal and kill and destroy; I came that they may have life, and have it abundantly."

[14] American Psychological Association. "Stress in America Findings" November 9, 2010.

[15] Matlack, Jennifer. "Erase Stress for Good." Jan 2011. Better Homes and Gardens. www.bhg.com

[16] Luke 4:23 – "Jesus said to them, 'Surely you will quote this proverb to me: "Physician, heal yourself! Do here in your hometown what we have heard that you did in Capernaum."""

[17] Aslan's Place Ministries website: www.aslansplace.org

[18] Thriving: Recover Your Life website: www.thrivingrecovery.org

[19] The Life Model website: www.lifemodel.org

[20] Equipping Hearts for the Harvest website: www.equippinghearts.com

[21] Friesen, James G., Wilder, E. James, Bierling Anne M., Koepcke, Rick, and Maribeth Poole. *Life Model, Living from the Heart that Jesus Gave You.* Shepherds House Inc. 1999.

[22] See Deuteronomy 30:29 and Proverbs 18:21

[23] Psalm 121:4

Ministering Over Trauma in Children

[24] More information about Sozo ministry can be found in Andy Reese's Book, Freedom Tools, by visiting

http://www.thefreedomresource.org/, or by going to http://www.bethelsozo.com/

25 The Immanuel Method is based on the reality that God is always present with us and always has been (Deut 31:8, Matt 28:20, Heb 13:5). For more information go to http://www.lifemodel.org/download.php?type=diagram &rn=173

26 John 20:23 – "If you forgive anyone his sins, they are forgiven; if you do not forgive them, they are not forgiven."

Trauma Prayer for Victims of Trafficking

27 A "John" is a person who hires a prostitute.

Ministering to the Homeless

28 National Law Center On Homelessness And Poverty, 2007 Annual Report

29 "Florida Department of Veteran's Administration Veteran's Statistics." May 2008. Florida Department of Veterans Affairs, Tallahassee, and Benderley, Beryl Lieff, "Veterans and Their Families, A SAMHSA Priority," Substance Abuse and Mental Health Services Administration News, January/February 2008, Volume 16, Number 1. For additional information see: www.awalkforthehomeless.net & www.homeaid.org

30 "Homelessness." June 11, 2009. Substance Abuse and Mental Health Services Administration, Center for Mental Health Services. http://mentalhealth.samhsa.gov/cmhs/Homelessness/

31 See Luke 14:23; Matthew 22:9

Ministering to Returning War Veterans

32 Homelessness among Veterans, 2005. Available at http://www1.va.gov

33 Roehr, Bob. "High Rate of PTSD in Returning Iraq War Veterans." http://www.medscape.com/viewarticle/565407 Medscape Medical News. 2007

34 Please note: in no way are we saying that the people who currently inhabit those lands are all "cursed" with these oppressions. Also, we are not saying that one must view these peoples through these powers/principalities to receive freedom.

35 Proverbs 16:18 (NASB)

36 See Isaiah 16:6; 25:11

37 Genesis 19:38 – "The younger daughter also had a son, and she named him Ben-Ammi; he is the father of the Ammonites of today.

38 Daniel 10:13 – "But the prince of the Persian kingdom resisted me twenty-one days. Then Michael, one of the chief princes, came to help me, because I was detained there with the king of Persia."

39 See also Genesis 19:38, Deuteronomy 3:11, Judges 10:7; 11:40

Name Definitions collected from: Hitchcock, Roswell D. *Hitchcock's Bible Names Dictionary.* Benediction Classics. May 2, 2010

Ungodly Ties of the Soul

40 "Facebook is a social network service and website launched in February 2004 that is operated and privately owned by Facebook, Inc. As of January 2011, Facebook has more than 600 million active users. Users may create a personal profile, add other users as friends and exchange messages, including automatic notifications when they update their profile. Additionally, users may join common interest user groups, organized by workplace, school, or college, or other characteristics. The name of the service stems from the colloquial name for the book

given to students at the start of the academic year by university administrations in the US with the intention of helping students to get to know each other better. Facebook allows anyone who declares themselves to be at least 13 years old to become a registered user of the website." "Facebook." Wikipedia, The Free Encyclopedia. Wikimedia Foundation, Inc. 30 January 2011.

[41] Ephesians 5:31 (see also Genesis 2:24) - "For this reason a man will leave his father and mother and be united to his wife, and the two will become one flesh."

Love: The Greater Force

[42] The Parable of the Rich Young Ruler (Luke 18:18-23)

[43] John 1:1; 14 – "In the beginning was the Word, and the Word was with God, and the Word was God. The Word became flesh and made his dwelling among us. We have seen his glory, the glory of the One and Only, who came from the Father, full of grace and truth."

[44] Revelation 13:8b – ". . .belonging to the Lamb that was slain from the creation of the world."

[45] Romans 5:8 – "But God demonstrates his own love for us in this: While we were still sinners, Christ died for us."

[46] I Corinthians 13:13 – "And now these three remain: faith, hope and love. But the greatest of these is love."

[47] Revelation 5:9-10. Full text: "And they sang a new song: "You are worthy to take the scroll and to open its seals, because you were slain, and with your blood you purchased men for God from every tribe and language and people and nation.

"You have made them to be a kingdom and priests to serve our God, and they will reign on the earth." See also Genesis 22; Revelation 13:8b

[48] John 15:13 – "Greater love has no one than this, that he lay down his life for his friends."

49 John 17:4 – "I have brought you glory on earth by completing the work you gave me to do."

John 19:30 – "When he had received the drink, Jesus said, 'It is finished.' With that, he bowed his head and gave up his spirit."

www.houseofhealingministries.org

Visit our website for more Resources, Ministry Tools, Schedules of Events, and more.

And soon to come – more publications by *House of Healing Ministries!*